GOD'S STORY
your story
YOUTH EDITION

To Brandon
from Brian
YFCamp 2012

Please pass this on
to Elijah when
you're done.

GOD'S STORY
your story
YOUTH EDITION

WHEN HIS BECOMES YOURS

MAX LUCADO
Adapted by Mark Matlock

ZONDERVAN.com/
AUTHORTRACKER
follow your favorite authors

ZONDERVAN

God's Story, Your Story: Youth Edition
Copyright © 2011 by Max Lucado

This title is also available as a Zondervan ebook. Visit www.zondervan.com/ebooks.

This title is also available in a Zondervan audio edition. Visit www.zondervan.fm.

Requests for information should be addressed to:

Zondervan, *Grand Rapids, Michigan* 49530

Library of Congress Cataloging-in-Publication Data

Matlock, Mark.
      God's story, your story : when His becomes yours / Max Lucado ; teen adaptation by Mark
Matlock. — Youth ed.
            p.   cm.
      Includes bibliographical references.
      ISBN 978-0-310-72546-6 (softcover)
      1. Christian teenagers — Religious life. 2. Christian life. I. Lucado, Max. God's story, your
story. II. Title.
BV4531.3.M38155 2011
248.8'3 — dc23   2011018463

Cover design: The A Group
Interior design: Beth Shagene

Printed in the United States of America

---

11 12 13 14 15 16 17 18 /DCI/ 23 22 21 20 19 18 17 16 15 14 13 12 11 10 9 8 7 6 5 4 3 2 1

For Brett—

dear friend, brother, and son-in-law. Love you!

GOD rewrote the text of my life
when I opened the book of my heart to his eyes.

2 SAMUEL 22:25 MSG

CONTENTS

ACKNOWLEDGMENTS

If these acknowledgments were posted on *Facebook*, these special folks would rate a "like":

Mark Matlock and his youth group — your compelling stories added just the right "teen touch" to this volume. I'm grateful to each of you!

Jacque Alberta and the Zondervan team — I'm applauding your expertise and careful shepherding of this book.

Shelby Di Giosia and Joshua Padilla — thanks for sharing your youthful perspective. Good job!

WHEN GOD'S STORY BECOMES YOURS ...

THE LOCAL COMMUNITY THEATER GROUP WAS STAGING the play *The Wizard of Oz*, and they needed some Munchkins. They recruited the children's choir (in which I sang second soprano, thank you very much) to play the parts. We learned the songs and practiced the dances, but our choir director overlooked one detail. He never told us the story. He assumed we'd seen the movie. I hadn't. As far as I knew, Toto was a chocolate candy, and the Yellow Brick Road was an avenue in Disneyland. I knew nothing of Kansas tornadoes or hot-air balloons. I didn't know how the story started or ended, but I found myself in the middle of it.

Dress rehearsal nearly did me in. A house crashed out of the sky. A queen floated in a bubble. A long-nosed witch waved her stick. "I'll get you, my pretty ..." I was wide-eyed and wondering what I'd gotten myself into. Life in Munchkinland can be a scary thing.

Unless you've read the screenplay. Unless you know the final act. When you enter the stage equipped with a script, everything changes. You know that in the end the witch melts. So let her cackle all she wants; her days are numbered. In the end, good wins.

Everything changes when you know the rest of your story.

As David discovered, "God rewrote the text of my life when I opened the book of my heart to his eyes" (2 Samuel 22:25 MSG). But what is the text of our lives?

The question is not a new one. Self-help gurus, talk show hosts, and magazine headlines urge you to find your narrative. But they send you in the wrong direction. "Look inside yourself," they say. But the promise of self-discovery falls short. Can you find the plot of a book in one paragraph or hear the flow of a symphony in one measure? Can you uncover the plot of your life by examining your life? By no means. You are so much more than a few days between the womb and the tomb.

Your story indwells God's. This is the great promise of the Bible and the hope of this book. "It's in Christ that we find out who we are and what we are living for. Long before we first heard of Christ and got our hopes up, he had his eye on us, had designs on us for glorious living, part of the overall purpose he is working out in everything and everyone" (Ephesians 1:11–12 MSG).

Above and around us God directs a grander saga, written by his hand, orchestrated by his will, unveiled according to his calendar. And you are a part of it. Meaningless Munchkin? Not you. Stranded on the prairie in a creaky old farmhouse? No way. Your life emerges from the greatest mind and the kindest heart in the history of the universe: the mind and heart of God. "He makes everything work out according to his plan" (Ephesians 1:11 NLT).

Let's dive into his story, shall we? Our plan is simple: journey though the New Testament in search of God's narrative. We'll use the chronological Bible *The Story* as our guidebook, extracting a promise from each of its ten chapters.

Who knows? In his story we might find our own.

Max

CHAPTER 1

WHEN GOD'S STORY BECOMES YOURS ...

ORDINARY MATTERS

THINK ABOUT IT!

Every great story starts with ordinary people. Spider-Man was just Peter Parker, an ordinary kid in love with the girl next door. Luke Skywalker was a farmer on the planet of Tatooine before he found the message from a princess in need of rescue. Cinderella was just a poor girl living at the whims of an evil parent. But extraordinary stories come from ordinary people. And extraordinary is exactly what happens when God's story meets ours.

Do you believe that God may want to do something incredible in your life?

THE PINT-SIZE JOSEPH SCURRIES ACROSS THE CHURCH
stage, wearing sandals, a robe, and his best attempt at an
anxious face. He raps on the door his dad built for the
children's Christmas play, then shifts from one foot to the
other, partly because he's supposed to act nervous. Mostly
because he is exactly that.

The innkeeper answers. He too wears a tow sack of a
robe and a towel turned turban. An elastic band secures
a false beard to his face. He looks at Joseph and chokes
back a giggle. Just a couple of hours ago the two boys were
building a front-lawn snowman. Their moms had to tell
them twice to get dressed for the Christmas Eve service.

Here they stand. The innkeeper crosses his arms;
Joseph waves his. He describes a donkey ride from

Nazareth, five days on the open road, a census here in Bethlehem, and, most of all, a wife. He turns and points in the direction of a pillow-stuffed nine-year-old girl.

She waddles onto center stage with one hand on the small of her back and the other mopping her brow. She limps with her best portrayal of pregnant pain, though, if pressed, she would have no clue about the process of childbirth.

She plays up the part. Groan. Sigh. "Joseph, I need help!"

The crowd chuckles.

Joseph looks at the innkeeper.

The innkeeper looks at Mary.

And we all know what happens next. Joseph urges. The innkeeper shakes his head. His hotel is packed. Guests occupy every corner. There is no room at the inn.

I think some dramatic license could be taken here. Rather than hurry to the next scene, let Joseph plead his case. "Mr. Innkeeper, think twice about your decision. Do you know whom you are turning away? That's God inside that girl! You're closing the door on the King of the universe. Better reconsider. Do you really want to be memorialized as the person who turned out heaven's child into the cold?"

And let the innkeeper react. "I've heard some desperate appeals for a room, but *God inside a girl?* That girl? She's got pimples and puffy ankles, for goodness' sake! Doesn't look like a God-mother to me. And you don't look too special yourself there … uh … What was your name? Oh yeah, Joe. Good ol' Joe. Covered head to toe with road dust. Take your tale somewhere else, buddy. I'm not falling for your story. Sleep in the barn for all I care!"

The innkeeper huffs and turns. Joseph and Mary exit. The choir sings "Away in a Manger" as stagehands wheel out a pile of hay, a feed trough, and some plastic sheep. The audience smiles and claps and sings along. They love the song, the kids, and they cherish the story. But most of all, they cling to the hope. The Christmas hope that God indwells the everydayness of our world.

The story drips with normalcy. This isn't *Queen* Mary or *King* Joseph. The couple doesn't caravan into Bethlehem with camels, servants, purple banners, and dancers. Mary and Joseph have no money or political pull. They have the clout of a migrant worker and the net worth of a minimum wage earner.

Not subjects for a PBS documentary.

Not candidates for welfare either. Their life is difficult but not destitute. Joseph has the means to pay taxes. They live in that populous world between royalty and rubes.

They are, well, normal. Normal has calluses like

Joseph, stretch marks like Mary. Normal stays up late getting homework done and wakes up early for classes. Normal is Norm and Norma, not Prince and Princess.

Norm sings off-key. Norma works at Chik-fil-A and struggles to find time to pray. Both have stood where Joseph stood and have heard what Mary heard. Not from the innkeeper in Bethlehem, but from the coach in middle school or the hunk in high school. "We don't have room for you ... time for you ... a space for you ... a job for you ... interest in you. Besides, look at you. You are too slow ... fat ... inexperienced ... late ... young ... old ... pigeon-toed ... cross-eyed ... zit-faced. You are too ... ordinary."

But then comes the Christmas story, Norm and Norma from Normal, Ohio, plodding into ho-hum Bethlehem in the middle of the night. No one notices them. No one looks twice in their direction. The innkeeper won't even clean out a corner in the attic. Trumpets don't blast; bells don't sound; angels don't toss confetti. Aren't we glad they didn't?

What if Joseph and Mary had shown up in designer clothes with a chauffeur, bling-blinged and high-muckety-mucked? And what if God had decked out Bethlehem like Hollywood on Oscar night: red carpet, flashing lights, with angels interviewing the royal couple? "Mary, Mary, you look simply divine."

Had Jesus come with such whoop-de-do, we would have read the story and thought, My, *look how Jesus entered their world.*

But since he didn't, we can read the story and dream. My, *might Jesus be born in my world? My everyday world?*

Lydia, 18 — It's cool how Jesus started off with an "ordinary" life. Yeah, he didn't sin, but he didn't appear to have superfancy talents until he turned water into wine.

It's the small things that make a big difference. Like earlier when my friend thanked me for doing something for them.

Jesus would *not* be the same if he was a superstar. Duh. Superstars do not equal normal people. If Jesus was a superstar, he can't say he faced all the trials we faced — he wouldn't seem so legit.

Of course, most of us teenagers don't like being considered "ordinary"; everyone wants to have a unique identity.

Isn't that where you live? Not a holiday world. Or a red-letter-day world. No, you live an everyday life. You have bills to pay, beds to make, and grass to cut. Your face won't grace any magazine covers, and you aren't expecting a call from the White House. Congratulations. You qualify for a modern-day Christmas story. God enters the world through folks like you and comes on days like today.

The splendor of the first Christmas is the lack thereof.

Step into the stable, and cradle in your arms the infant Jesus, still moist from the womb, just wrapped in the rags. Run a finger across his chubby cheek, and listen as one who knew him well puts lyrics to the event:

"In the beginning was the Word" (John 1:1).

The words "In the beginning" take us to the beginning. "In the beginning God created the heavens and the earth" (Genesis 1:1). The baby Mary held was connected to the dawn of time. He saw the first ray of sunlight and heard the first crash of a wave. The baby was born, but the Word never was.

"All things were made through him" (1 Corinthians 8:6 NCV). Not *by* him, but *through* him. Jesus didn't fashion the world out of raw material he found. He created all things out of nothing.

Jesus: the Genesis Word, "the firstborn over all creation" (Colossians 1:15). He is the "one Lord, Jesus Christ, through whom God made everything and through whom we have been given life" (1 Corinthians 8:6 NLT).

And then, what no theologian conceived, what no

rabbi dared to dream, God did. "The Word became flesh" (John 1:14). The Artist became oil on his own palette. The Potter melted into the mud on his own wheel. God became an embryo in the belly of a village girl. Christ in Mary. God in Christ.

Astounding, this thought of heaven's fetus floating within the womb. Joseph and Mary didn't have the advantage we have: ultrasound. When my wife, Denalyn, was pregnant with each of our three daughters, we took full advantage of the technology. The black-and-white image on the screen looked more like Doppler radar than a child. But with the help of the doctor, we were able to see the arms and hands and the pierced nose and prom dress ... Wait, I'm confusing photos.

As the doctor moved the instrument around Denalyn's belly, he took inventory. "There's the head, the feet, the torso ... Well, everything looks normal."

Mary's doctor would have made the same announcement. Jesus was an ordinary baby. There is nothing in the story to imply that he levitated over the manger or walked out of the stable. Just the opposite. He "dwelt among us" (John 1:14 NKJV). John's word for *dwelt* traces its origin to *tabernacle* or *tent*. Jesus did not separate himself from his creation; he pitched his tent in the neighborhood.

The Word of God entered the world with the cry of

a baby. His family had no cash or connections or strings to pull. Jesus, the Maker of the universe, the one who invented time and created breath, was born into a family too humble to swing a bed for a pregnant mom-to-be.

God writes his story with people like Joseph and Mary ... and Sam Stone.

In the weeks before Christmas 1933, a curious offer appeared in the daily newspaper of Canton, Ohio. "Man Who Felt Depression's Sting to Help 75 Unfortunate Families." A Mr. B. Virdot promised to send a check to the neediest in the community. All they had to do was describe their plight in a letter and mail it to General Delivery.

The plunging economy had left fathers with no jobs, houses with no heat, children with patched clothing, and an entire nation, it seemed, with no hope.

The appeals poured in.

"I hate to write this letter ... it seems too much like begging ... my husband doesn't know I'm writing ... He is working but not making enough to hardly feed his family."

"Mr. Virdot, we are in desperate circumstances ... No one knows, only those who go through it."

All of Canton knew of Mr. Virdot's offer. Oddly, no one knew Mr. Virdot. The city registry of 105,000 citizens contained no such name. People wondered if he really existed. Yet within a week checks began to arrive at homes all over the area. Most were modest, about five dollars. All were signed "B. Virdot."

Through the years, the story was told, but the identity of the man was never discovered. In 2008, long after his death, a grandson opened a tattered black suitcase that had collected dust in his parents' attic. That's where he found the letters, all dated in December 1933, as well as 150 canceled checks. Mr. B. Virdot was Samuel J. Stone. His pseudonym was a hybrid of Barbara, Virginia, and Dorothy, the names of his three daughters.[1]

There was nothing privileged about Sam Stone. If anything, his upbringing was marred by challenge. He was fifteen when his family emigrated from Romania. They settled into a Pittsburgh ghetto, where his father hid Sam's shoes so he couldn't go to school and forced him and his six siblings to roll cigars in the attic.

Still, Stone persisted. He left home to work on a barge, then in a coal mine, and by the time the Depression hit, he owned a small chain of clothing stores and lived in relative comfort. He wasn't affluent, or impoverished, but he was willing to help.

Ordinary man. Ordinary place. But a conduit of extraordinary grace. And in God's story, ordinary matters.

DON'T JUST SIT THERE ...

Thank God for sending Jesus as an ordinary person into an everyday family so he can understand what it's like to be human.

Make a quick list of three of your best friends. What makes them ordinary? Does that keep them from mattering to you?

Ask God to help you to trust him to use your ordinary life to do good things.

Ask a good friend to tell you the story of their life. Notice how they see their part in it.

If your parents are Christians, ask them to tell you the story of how they came to trust in Jesus.

CHAPTER 2

WHEN GOD'S STORY
BECOMES YOURS ...

YOU KNOW
SATAN'S NEXT
MOVE

THINK ABOUT IT!

Every story has a bad guy. They may be as bold as Darth Vader, Lord Voldemort, or the Joker. Villains can also be subtler, like a jealous friend, a clueless principal, or a cheating competitor. They are the ones who keep our hero from accomplishing his mission, his purpose in the story. The hero learns and grows as he struggles to be victorious over his adversaries. God's story tells us that we too have an enemy, Satan. But it also tells us how we can defeat him and grow tremendously when we encounter his tricks and snares in life.

I F I WERE THE DEVIL, I'D BE TICKED OFF. TICKED OFF TO see you reading a Christian book, thinking godly thoughts, dreaming about heaven and other such blah-blah-blah.

How dare you ponder God's story! What about my story? I had my eyes on you . . . had plans for you. That's what I would think.

If I were the devil, I'd get busy. I'd assemble my minions and demons into a strategy session and give them your picture and address. I'd review your weaknesses one by one. *Don't think I don't know them. How you love to be liked and hate to be wrong. How cemeteries give you the creeps and darkness gives you the heebie-jeebies.*

I'd brief my staff on my past victories. *Haven't I had my share? Remember your bouts with doubt? I all but had you* convinced that the Bible was a joke. You and your so-called faith in God's Word.

I'd stealth my way into your mind. No frontal attacks for you. Witchcraft and warlocks won't work with your type. No. If I were the devil, I'd dismantle you with questions. How do you know, I mean, truly know, that Jesus rose from the dead? Are you sure you really believe the gospel? Isn't absolute truth yesterday's news? You, a child of God? Come on.

I might direct you to one of my churches. One of my "feel good, you're good, everything's good" churches. Half Hollywood, half pep talk. Glitz, lights, and love. But no talk of Jesus. No mention of sin, hell, or forgiveness. I'd suffocate you with promises of pay raises and new cars. Then again, you're a bit savvy for that strategy.

Distraction would work better. I hate spiritual focus. When you or one like you gazes intently on God for any length of time, you begin to act like him. A nauseating sense of justice and virtue comes over you. You talk to God, not just once a week, but all of the time. Intolerable.

So I'd perch myself on every corner and stairwell of your world, clamoring for your attention. I'd flood you with emails and to-do lists. Entice you with shopping sprees and latest releases and newest styles. Burden you with deadlines and assignments.

If I were the devil, I'd so distract you with possessions and problems that you'd never have time to read the Bible. Especially the story of Jesus in the wilderness. *What a disaster that day was! Jesus brought me down. Coldcocked me. Slam-dunked one right over my head. He knocked my best pitch over the Green Monster. I never even landed a punch. Looking back, I now realize what he was doing. He was making a statement. He wanted the whole world to know who calls the shots in the universe.*

If I were the devil, I wouldn't want you to read about the encounter. So, for that reason alone, let's do.

Then Jesus was led by the Spirit into the wilderness to be tempted by the devil. After fasting forty days and forty nights, he was hungry. The tempter came to him and said, "If you are the Son of God, tell these stones to become bread."

Jesus answered, "It is written: 'Man shall not live on bread alone, but on every word that comes from the mouth of God.'"

Then the devil took him to the holy city and had him stand on the highest point of the temple. "If you are the Son of God," he said, "throw yourself down. For it is written:

"'He will command his angels concerning you,
  and they will lift you up in their hands,
  so that you will not strike your foot against a
  stone.'"

Jesus answered him, "It is also written: 'Do not put the Lord your God to the test.'"

Again, the devil took him to a very high mountain and showed him all the kingdoms of the world and their splendor. "All this I will give you," he said, "if you will bow down and worship me."

Jesus said to him, "Away from me, Satan! For it is written: 'Worship the Lord your God, and serve him only.'"

Then the devil left him, and angels came and attended him.

—MATTHEW 4:1–11

Dorothy, 16—When Jesus was tempted in the wilderness, Satan had obviously thought about his attack. Satan was really clever, but no match for Jesus. I loved how Satan quoted out of the Bible; I honestly laughed to myself. Satan thinks he can tempt Jesus Christ, the one and only Son of God? Did he not get that? The Son of God! Wow, Satan really didn't get it.

Jesus was fresh out of the Jordan River. He had just been baptized by John the Baptist. At his baptism he had been affirmed by God with a dove and a voice: "You are my Son, whom I love; with you I am well pleased" (Luke 3:22). He stepped out of the waters buoyed by God's blessing. Yet he began his public ministry, not by healing the sick or preaching a sermon, but by exposing the scheme of Satan. A perfect place to begin.

How do we explain our badness? Our stubborn hearts and hurtful hands and conniving ways? How do we explain Auschwitz, human trafficking, abuse? Trace malevolence upriver to its beginning, where will the river take us? What will we see?

If I were the devil, I'd blame evil on a broken political system. A crippled economy. The roll of the dice. The Wicked Witch of the West. I'd want you to feel attacked by an indefinable, nebulous force. After all, if you can't diagnose the source of your ills, how can you treat them? If I were the devil, I'd keep my name out of it.

But God doesn't let the devil get away with this and tells us his name. The Greek word for devil is *diabolos*, which shares a root with the verb *diaballein*, which means "to split." The devil is a splitter, a divider, a wedge driver. He divided Adam and Eve from God in the garden, and has every intent of doing the same to you. Blame all unrest on him. Don't fault the plunging economy or a society that doesn't "get" teenagers for your anxiety. They are simply tools in Satan's tool kit. He is the

- serpent (Genesis 3:14; Revelation 12:9; 20:2)

- tempter (Matthew 4:3; 1 Thessalonians 3:5)

- enemy (Matthew 13:25, 39)

- evil one (Matthew 13:19; 1 John 2:13 – 14)

- prince of demons (Mark 3:22)

- father of lies (John 8:44)

- murderer (John 8:44)

- roaring lion (1 Peter 5:8)

- deceiver (Revelation 12:9 GWT)

- dragon (Revelation 12:7, 9; 20:2)

Satan is not absent from or peripheral to God's story. He is at its center. We can't understand God's narrative without understanding Satan's strategy. In fact, "the reason the Son of God appeared was to destroy the works of the devil" (1 John 3:8 ESV).

Nothing thrills Satan more than the current skepticism with which he is viewed. When people deny his existence or chalk up his works to the ills of society, he rubs his hands with glee. The more we doubt his very existence, the more he can work without hindrance.

Jesus didn't doubt the reality of the devil. The Savior strode into the badlands with one goal, to unmask Satan, and made him the first stop on his itinerary. "Then Jesus was led by the Spirit into the wilderness to be tempted by the devil" (Matthew 4:1).

Does God do the same with us? Might the Spirit of God lead us into the wilderness? If I were the devil, I'd tell you no. I would want you to think that I, on occasion, snooker heaven. That I catch God napping. That I sneak in when he isn't looking and snatch his children out of his hand. I'd leave you sleeping with one eye open.

But Scripture reveals otherwise. The next time you hear the phrase "all hell broke loose," correct the speaker. Hell does not break loose. God uses Satan's temptation to strengthen us. (If I were the devil, that would aggravate me to no end.) Times of testing are actually times of training, purification, and strength building. You can even "consider it pure joy ... whenever you face trials of many kinds, because you know that the testing of your faith produces perseverance" (James 1:2–3).

God loves you too much to leave you undeveloped and immature. "God disciplines us for our own good, that we may share in his holiness. No discipline seems pleasant at the time, but painful. Later on, however, it produces a harvest of righteousness and peace for those who have been trained by it" (Hebrews 12:10–11). Expect to be tested by the devil.

And watch for his tricks. You can know what to expect. "We are not ignorant of his schemes" (2 Corinthians 2:11 NASB).

When General George Patton counterattacked Field Marshal Rommel in World War II, he is reported to have shouted in the thick of battle, "I read your book, Rommel! I read your book!" Patton had studied Rommel's *Infantry Attacks*. He knew the German leader's strategy and planned his moves accordingly.[2] We can know the same about the devil.

We know Satan will *attack weak spots first*. Forty days of fasting left Jesus famished, so Satan began with the topic of bread. Jesus' stomach was empty, so to the stomach Satan turned.

Where are you empty? Are you hungry for attention, craving success, longing for intimacy? Be aware of your weaknesses. Bring them to God before Satan brings them to you. Satan will tell you to turn stones into bread (Matthew 4:3). In other words, *meet your own needs*, take matters into your own hands, leave God out of the picture.

Whereas Jesus teaches us to pray for bread (Matthew 6:11), Satan says to work for bread.

Besides, he said, "If you are the Son of God" (Matthew 4:3), you can do this. Ah, another ploy: *raise a question about identity.* Make Christians think they have to prove their position with rock-to-bread miracles. Clever. If Satan convinces us to trust our works over God's Word, he has us dangling from a broken limb. Our works will never hold us.

Jesus didn't even sniff the bait. Three times he repeated, "It is written ..."; "It is also written ..."; "It is written ..." (verses 4, 7, 10). In his book, God's book was enough. He overcame temptation, not with special voices or supernatural signs, but by remembering and quoting Scripture.

(If I were the devil, I wouldn't want you to underline that sentence.)

Satan regrouped and tried a different approach. This one may surprise you. He told Jesus to *show off in church.* "Then the devil took him to the holy city and had him stand on the highest point of the temple. 'If you are the Son of God,' he said, 'throw yourself down'" (verses 5–6).

Testing isn't limited to the desert; it also occurs in the sanctuary. The two stood on the southeastern wall of the temple, more than a hundred feet above the Kidron

Valley, and Satan told Jesus to jump into the arms of God. Jesus refused, not because he couldn't, not because God wouldn't catch him. He refused because he didn't have to prove anything to anyone, much less the devil.

Neither do you. Satan is going to tell you otherwise. In church, of all places, he will urge you to do tricks: impress others with your service, make a show of your faith, call attention to your good deeds. He loves to turn church assemblies into Las Vegas presentations where people show off their abilities rather than boast in God's. Don't be suckered.

Satan's last shot began with a mountain climb. "The devil took him to a very high mountain" (verse 8). Another note out of Satan's playbook: *promise heights.* Promise the highest place, the first place, the peak, the pinnacle. The best, the most, the top. These are Satan's favorite words. The devil led Jesus higher and higher, hoping, I suppose, that the thin air would confuse his thinking. He "showed [Jesus] all the kingdoms of the world and their splendor. 'All this I will give you,' he said, 'if you will bow down and worship me'" (verses 8–9).

Oops. Satan just showed his cards. He wants worship. He wants you and me to tell him how great he is. He wants to write his own story in which he is the hero and God is an afterthought. He admitted as much:

"I will ascend to the heavens;
I will raise my throne
above the stars of God;
I will sit enthroned on the mount of assembly,
on the utmost heights of Mount Zaphon.
I will ascend above the tops of the clouds;
I will make myself like the Most High."

—ISAIAH 14:13–14

Satan wants to take God's place, but God isn't moving. Satan covets the throne of heaven, but God isn't leaving. Satan wants to win you to his side, but God will never let you go.

You have his word. Even more, you have God's help.

For our high priest [Jesus] is able to understand our weaknesses. When he lived on earth, he was tempted in every way that we are, but he did not sin. Let us, then, feel very sure that we can come before God's throne where there is grace. There we can receive mercy and grace to help us when we need it.

—HEBREWS 4:15–16 NCV

The last two Greek words of that verse are *eukairon boçtheian*. *Eukarios* means "timely" or "seasonable" or "opportune." *Boçtheia* is a compound of *boç*, "to shout," and *theô*, "to run." Nice combination. We shout, and God runs at the right moment. God places himself prior to our need, and just before we encounter that need, he gives us what we need.

You don't have to face Satan alone. You know his schemes. He will attack your weak spots first. He will tell you to meet your own needs. When you question your identity as a child of God, that is Satan speaking. If you turn church into a talent show, now you know why.

Even more, now you know what to do.

Pray. We cannot do battle with Satan on our own. He is a roaring lion, a fallen angel, an experienced fighter, and a trained soldier. He is angry — angry because he knows that his time is short (Revelation 12:12) and that God's victory is secure. He resents God's goodness toward us and our worship of God. He is a skillful, powerful, ruthless foe who seeks to "work us woe; His craft and power are great, and armed with cruel hate, on earth is not his equal."[3] But there is wonderful news for the Christian: Christ reigns as our protector and provider. We are more than conquerors through him (Romans 8:37).

Arm yourself with God's Word. Load your pistol with Scriptures and keep a finger on the trigger. And remember: "Our struggle is not against flesh and blood, but against the rulers, against the authorities, against the powers of this dark world and against the spiritual forces of evil in the heavenly realms" (Ephesians 6:12).

If I were the devil, I wouldn't want you to know that. But I'm not the devil, so good for you. And take that, Satan.

Lauren, 15 — Knowing Satan is real changes the way I live each day, because when you know that Satan's out to bring you down, then it gives you that much more reason to fight against him and focus on God's story for your life.

DON'T JUST SIT THERE . . .

Thank God that Jesus overcame Satan's temptations without using any superpowers—and that with God's help, you can too.

Make a quick list of your three most common cravings (e.g., food, sex, popularity, revenge, doing nothing, etc.). Circle the one you think Satan might most effectively use against you to get you to make a foolish or sinful choice.

Ask a Christian friend you can trust to go through your list with you and talk together about some of the ways Satan might tempt you to make stupid choices.

Text or Facebook (or email or whatever) this to a Christian friend today: "Tell me one thing you know for sure is true from the Bible."

Ask your parent or youth leader or another wise Christian to suggest a passage you could memorize and say to yourself when tempted to do that thing you are most often tempted to do.

Memorize that passage!

CHAPTER 3

WHEN GOD'S STORY
BECOMES YOURS ...

YOU FIND
YOUR TRUE
HOME

THINK ABOUT IT!

One of the best-loved stories ever is about a little girl who gets caught in a tornado and finds herself in a strange and colorful land called Oz. Have you ever watched the 1939 film *The Wizard of Oz*? Though the place is as brightly colored as a dream and filled with extraordinary characters, Dorothy has just one mission in Oz: to get back home to Kansas.

In a way, every story is about getting home, finding a home, or fixing something to make it the way it should be at home. Home is the place where you hope to find truth and justice and happiness and family. And love, of course.

Heroes are often driven to make things right (or escape what's wrong). Good stories show heroes trying to make the world they live in better homes for themselves or others.

Your part in God's story is a lot like that too. None of us are home yet. And we'll never find the home we dream of in this life. Our only hope for the perfect home, the perfect family, the perfect love is in the life to come when we'll finally be reunited with our Father.

For all we don't know about Mr. Holden Howie, of one thing we can be certain. He knew his birds would find their way home. Several times a day the square-bodied, gray-bearded New Zealander retrieved one of his pigeons from his Auckland aviary. Securing the feathered courier with one hand, he affixed the correspondence with the other. Some birds carried as many as five messages at a time, each one written on cigarette paper. Mr. Howie then released the bird into the South Pacific sky. It flew straight as a string to its nest on Great Barrier Island.[4]

Between 1898 and 1908, Mr. Howie delivered thousands of messages. His birds were speedy. They could travel in two hours the distance a boat would traverse in three days. Dependable. Storms rarely knocked the pigeons off course, and they never called in sick. And, most notably, they were accurate. They could find their nest. Why else would we call them homing pigeons?

Other birds fly faster. Other birds are stronger. Other birds boast larger plumes or stronger claws. But none have the navigational skill of the homing pigeon.

Some scientists believe pigeons have traces of magnetite in their beaks and brains that interplay with the magnetic field of the earth.[5] Others credit the birds' sense of hearing. Do they pick up a frequency other birds miss? Or do they sniff out their target with a keen sense of smell?

What we know is this: pigeons have an innate home detector.

So do you.

What God gave pigeons, he gave to you. No, not bird brains. A guidance system. You were born heaven equipped with a hunger for your heavenly home. Need proof?

Consider your questions. Questions about death and time, significance and relevance. Animals don't seem to ask the questions we do. Dogs howl at the moon, but we stare at it. How did we get here? What are we here for? Are we someone's idea or something's accident? Why on earth are we on this earth?

Brendon, 16—Sometimes I find myself like the homing pigeon, wanting to fly straight to my destination, which is heaven, where there is no sin, there are perfect families, and where I can sit right next to Jesus Christ. But I find myself getting stuck in storms, like when I'm home with my broken family and sin all around me. But I am able to stay focused on my heavenly home while I'm here on my mission trying to lead my family and friends to Christ so they can fix their eyes on a greater and perfect earth.

We ask questions about pain. The words *leukemia* and *child* shouldn't appear in the same sentence. And war. Can't conflict go the way of phonograph records and telegrams? And the grave. Why is the dash between the dates on a tombstone so small? Something tells us this isn't right, good, fair. This isn't home.

From whence come these stirrings? Who put these thoughts in our heads? Why can't we, like rabbits, be happy with carrots and copulation? Because, according to Jesus, we aren't home yet.

Probably his best-known story follows the trail of a homeless runaway. Jesus doesn't give us a name, just a pedigree: rich. Donald Trump rich. Paris Hilton spoiled rich. A silver-spooned, yacht-owning, trust-funded, blue-blooded boy. Rather than learn his father's business, he disregarded his father's kindness, cashed in his stock, and drove his Mercedes to the big city.

As fast as you can say dead broke, he was exactly that. No friends, no funds, no clue what to do. He ended up in a pigpen of trouble. He fed hogs, slept in the mud, and grew so hungry he gave serious consideration to licking the slop. That's when he thought of home. He remembered lasagna, popcorn in the microwave, and family movie night. His warm bed, clean pajamas, and fuzzy slippers. He missed his father's face and longed for his father's voice. He looked around at the snorting pigs and buzzing flies and made a decision.

"I'll turn the pigpen into a home." He took out a loan from the piggy bank and remodeled the place. New throw rug over the mud. A La-Z-Boy recliner next to the trough. He hung a flat screen on the fence post, flipped the slop bucket upside down, and called it a lamp shade. He tied a ribbon on a sow's head and called her honey. He pierced the ear of a piglet and called him son. Within short order he'd made a home out of the pigsty and settled in for the good life.

Okay, maybe he didn't. But don't we? Don't we do our best to make this mess a home? Do up and doll up. Revamp and redecorate. We face-lift this. Overhaul that. Salt on the slop and whitewash for the posts. Ribbons for her and tattoos for him. And, in time, the place ain't half bad.

We actually feel at home.

But then the flies come out. People die, earthquakes come, and nations rage. Families collapse, and children die of hunger. Dictators snort and treat people like, well, like pigs. And this world stinks.

And we have a choice. We can pretend this life is all God intended. Or . . .

We can come to our senses. We can follow the example of the prodigal son. "I will set out and go back to my father" (Luke 15:18).

Don't you love the image of the son setting out for the homestead: rising out of the mud, turning his back to the pigs, and turning his eyes toward the father? This is Jesus' invitation to us. Set your hearts on your home. "Seek first the kingdom of God" (Matthew 6:33 NKJV).

In his plan it's all about the King and his kingdom. He wrote the script, built the sets, directs the actors, and knows the final act—an everlasting kingdom. "And this is [God's] plan: At the right time he will bring everything together under the authority of Christ—everything in heaven and on earth" (Ephesians 1:10 NLT).

Reach for it!

The journey home is nice, but the journey is not the

goal. I wrote part of this book on an airplane. As I looked around at fellow passengers, I saw content people. Thanks to books, pillows, and crossword puzzles, they passed the time quite nicely. But suppose this announcement were heard: "Ladies and Gentlemen, this flight is your final destination. We will never land. Your home is this plane, so enjoy the journey."

Passengers would become mutineers. We'd take over the cockpit and seek out a landing strip. We wouldn't settle for such an idea. The journey is not the destination. The vessel is not the goal. Those who are content with nothing more than joy in the journey are settling for too little satisfaction. Our hearts tell us there is more to this life than this life. We, like E.T., lift bent fingers to the sky. We may not know where to point, but we know not to call this airplane our home.

"God ... has placed eternity in the human heart" (Ecclesiastes 3:11 NLT). Mr. Howie released his pigeons from Auckland, and God released his children from the cage of time. Our privilege is to keep flapping until we spot the island. Those who do will discover a spiritual cache, a treasure hidden in a field, a pearl of great value (Matthew 13:44 – 46). Finding the kingdom is like finding a winning lottery ticket in your sock drawer or locating the cover to the jigsaw puzzle box. "Oh, this is how it's going to look."

In God's story, life on earth is but the beginning: the first letter of the first sentence in the first chapter of the great story God is writing with your life.

You will do your best work in heaven. Do you regret something you've done that you can't seem to escape? So do I. We have an eternity to make up for lost time. Are you puzzled by the challenges of your days? Then see yourself as a diamond in the rough and God as a jeweler. He is polishing you for your place in his kingdom. Your biggest moments lie ahead, on the other side of the grave.

So "seek those things which are above, where Christ is, sitting at the right hand of God" (Colossians 3:1 NKJV). Scripture uses a starchy verb here. Zçteite ("to seek") is to "covet earnestly, strive after, to inquire for, desire, even require."

Seek heaven like a sailor seeks the coast or a pilot seeks the landing strip or a missile seeks heat. Head for home like a pigeon wings to the nest or the prodigal strode to his papa. "Think only about" it (3:2 NCV). "Keep your mind" on it (3:2 GWT). "Set your sights on the realities of heaven" (3:1 NLT). "Pursue the things over which Christ presides" (3:1 MSG). Obsess yourself with heaven!

And, for heaven's sake, don't settle for pigpens on earth.

I found myself saying something similar to my nephew and niece. I had taken them to the San Antonio Zoo, a perfect place for a three- and five-year-old to spend a Saturday afternoon. A veteran kid-guide, I knew the path to take. Start small and end wild. We began with the lowly, glass-caged reptiles. Next we oohed and aahed at the parrots and pink flamingos. We fed the sheep in the petting zoo and tossed crumbs to the fish in the pond. But all along I kept telling Lawson and Callie, "We're getting closer to the big animals. Elephants and tigers are just around the corner."

Finally we reached the Africa section. For full effect I told them to enter with their heads down and their eyes on the sidewalk. I walked them right up to the elephant fence.

And just when I was about to tell them to lift their eyes, Lawson made a discovery. "Look, a doodlebug!"

"Where?" Callie asked.

"Here!" He squatted down and placed the pellet-sized insect in the palm of his hand and began to roll it around.

"Let me see it!" Callie said.

I couldn't lure them away. "Hey, guys, this is the jungle section."

No response.

"Don't you want to see the wild animals?"

No, they focused on the bug. There we stood, elephants to our left, lions to our right, only a stone's throw from hippos and leopards, and what were they doing? Playing with a doodlebug.

Don't we all? Myriads of mighty angels encircle us, the presence of our Maker engulfs us, the witness of a thousand galaxies and constellations calls to us, the flowing tide of God's history carries us, the crowning of Christ as King of the universe awaits us, but we can't get our eyes off the doodlebugs of life: paychecks, gadgets, vacations, and weekends.

Open your eyes, Christ invites. *Lift up your gaze.* "Seek first the kingdom of God" (Matthew 6:33 NKJV). Limit your world to the doodlebugs of this life, and, mark it down, you will be disappointed. Limit your story to the days between your birth and death, and brace yourself for a sad ending. You were made for more than this life.

Five hundred years ago, sailors feared the horizon. Sail too far and risk falling off the edge, they reasoned. Common wisdom of the ancients warned against the unseen. So did the monument at the Strait of Gibraltar. At its narrowest margin, Spaniards erected a huge marker that bore in its stone the three-word Latin slogan *Ne plus ultra*, or "No more beyond."

But then came Christopher Columbus and the voyage of 1492. The discovery of the New World changed everything. Spain acknowledged this in its coins, which came to bear the slogan *Plus ultra*—"More beyond."[6]

Why don't you chisel the *no* off your future? God has set your heart on home. Keep flying until you reach it.

Mark, 16 — True happiness—that's a tricky thing. It's something everyone thirsts for but rarely experiences. True happiness honestly comes from God and nowhere else. We search for happiness in lonely places like drugs, sex, social class, our rank in school, money, and alcohol—it goes on and on. Those stories are not God's stories. God's story is the only one that brings lasting joy.

If happiness comes from God, we'll find real joy when we're home with him. Shazam!

DON'T JUST SIT THERE . . .

Thank God that this life is not your real life, that you have a home beyond this world where every broken thing will be perfect.

Make a quick list of five broken things that come with this life. Circle two that you will be most glad are not part of your real life in eternity with God.

Make a quick list of three things in this life that will be in heaven — but better there than they ever could be here.

Ask two good Christian friends if they ever day-dream about what life in heaven will be like. If they do, ask what kinds of things they imagine.

If your parent is a Christian, ask them to help you make a list of all the loved ones they expect to meet in heaven.

Write down Colossians 3:1–4. Stick it up some-place where you'll be forced to look at it every day for a week.

CHAPTER 4

WHEN GOD'S STORY
BECOMES YOURS ...

YOU HEAR
A VOICE
YOU CAN TRUST

THINK ABOUT IT!

Luke Skywalker had Obi-Wan Kenobi and Yoda. Daniel had Mr. Miyagi, Harry Potter had Dumbledore, Frodo had Gandalf, and Cinderella had a fairy godmother. The feature players in all our stories have good voices they can trust to guide them past their confusing times. So how do we know whom to listen to?

YOU THINK IT'S HARD TO WALK IN THE DARK? FIND IT DIF-ficult to navigate a room with the lights off or your eyes closed? Try flying a small plane at fifteen thousand feet. Blind.

Jim O'Neill did. Not that he intended to do so. The sixty-five-year-old pilot was forty minutes into a four-hour solo flight from Glasgow, Scotland, to Colchester, England, when his vision failed. He initially thought he had been blinded by the sun but soon realized it was much worse. "Suddenly I couldn't see the dials in front of me. It was just a blur. I was helpless."

He gave new meaning to the phrase "flying blind."

Turns out, he'd suffered a stroke. O'Neill groped and found the radio of his Cessna and issued a Mayday alert.

Paul Gerrard, a Royal Air Force Wing Commander who had just completed a training sortie nearby, was contacted by air traffic controllers and took off in O'Neill's direction. He found the plane and began talking to the stricken pilot.

The commander told O'Neill what to do. His instructions were reassuring and simple: "A gentle right turn, please. Left a bit. Right a bit." He hovered within five hundred feet of O'Neill, shepherding him toward the nearest runway. Upon reaching it, the two began to descend. When asked if he could see the runway below, O'Neill apologized, "No sir, negative." O'Neill would have to land the plane by faith, not by sight. He hit the runway but bounced up again. The same thing happened on the second attempt. But on the eighth try, the blinded pilot managed to make a near-perfect landing.[7]

Can you empathize with O'Neill? Most can. We've been struck at various times in our lives, paralyzed not by a stroke but by circumstance. A best friend stabbed you in the back, you didn't make the team, your parents separated. We've lost sight of any safe landing strip and, in desperation, issued our share of Mayday prayers. We know the fear of flying blind.

Unlike O'Neill, however, we hear more than one voice. Many voices besiege our cockpit. The talk show host urges us to worry. The news forecasts a meltdown. The pastor says pray; the professor says phooey. So many opinions! Lose weight. Eat less fat. Join our church. Stop eating meat. It's enough to make you cover your ears and run.

And what if you follow the wrong voice? What if you make the same mistake as the followers of self-help guru James Arthur Ray? He promised to help people achieve spiritual and financial wealth, asserting to "double, triple, even multiply by ten the size of your business."

He gave more than financial counsel to the more than fifty clients who crowded into his 415-square-foot sweat lodge in Sedona, Arizona. They had paid him between nine thousand and ten thousand dollars apiece for a five-day spiritual warrior retreat. The participants had fasted for thirty-six hours as part of a personal spiritual quest, then ate a breakfast buffet before entering the saunalike

Zach, 17—When I first moved from Atlanta, the first people to accept me at school were not the best at honoring God. When we hung out I was always pressured into things I knew weren't right. I can't say I have heard God's voice directly, but he has used others to help guide me. My father loves God very much and has always been someone I can listen to who will keep me from harming myself.

hut that afternoon. People were passing out and vomiting, but were still urged to stay in the lodge. Two hours later, three of them were dead.[8]

Oh, the voices. How do we select the right one?

A more important question cannot be asked. In fact, a form of the question was asked by Jesus himself: "Who do you say I am?" (Mark 8:29).

He had led his disciples into Caesarea Philippi. The region was to religion what Walmart is to shopping— every variety in one place. A center of Baal worship. An impressive temple of white marble dedicated to the godhead of Caesar. Shrines to the Syrian gods. Here Jesus, within earshot of every spiritual voice of his era, asked his followers:

> "Who do people say I am?"
> They replied, "Some say John the Baptist; others say Elijah; and still others, one of the prophets."
> "But what about you?" he asked. "Who do you say I am?"
> Peter answered, "You are the Messiah."
>
> —MARK 8:27–29

When it came to expressing the opinions of others, the disciples were chatty. Everyone spoke. But when it came to this personal question, only Peter replied. We do well to wonder why. Why only one answer? Was Peter so confident and quick that the others had no time to speak? Did Peter drown out the replies of everyone else?

"YOU ARE THE MESSIAH!"

Maybe Peter's confession echoed off the walls of the temples. Or perhaps it didn't.

Perhaps no one else spoke because no one else knew what to say. John ducked his eyes. Philip looked away. Andrew cleared his throat. Nathaniel kicked the dirt, then elbowed Peter. And Peter sighed. He looked at this lean-faced, homeless teacher from Nazareth and pondered the question, "Who do you say I am?"

It couldn't have been a new one for Peter. He must have asked it a thousand times: the night when Jesus walked off the beach into the bay without sinking, the day he turned a boy's lunch into an "all you can eat" buffet, the time he wove a whip and drove the swindlers out of the temple. *Who is this man?*

Peter had asked the question. So have millions of other people. All serious students of Christ, indeed students of life, have stood in their personal version of Caesarea Philippi and contrasted Jesus with the great philosophers of the world and heard him inquire, "Who do you say I am?"

"You're a decent fellow," some have answered. After all, if you can't like Jesus, can you like anyone? In Jesus, the poor found a friend, and the forgotten found an advocate. Jesus was nothing if not good. True blue. Solid. Dependable. Everyone's first choice for a best friend, right?

Sure, if you want a best friend who claims to be God on earth. For being such an affable sort, Jesus had a curious habit of declaring divinity.

His favorite self-designation was Son of Man. The title appears eighty-two times in the four gospels, only once by anyone other than Jesus.[9]

"The Son of Man has nowhere to lay His head" (Matthew 8:20 NKJV).

"The Son of Man must suffer many things" (Mark 8:31 NKJV).

"They will see the Son of Man coming" (Mark 13:26 NKJV).

First-century listeners found the claim outrageous. They were acquainted with its origin in Daniel 7. In his visions the prophet Daniel saw "One like the Son of Man, coming with the clouds of heaven! . . . Then to Him was given dominion and glory and a kingdom, that all peoples, nations, and languages should serve Him. His dominion is an everlasting dominion, which shall not pass away, and His kingdom the one which shall not be destroyed" (Daniel 7:13 – 14 NKJV).

"That's me," Jesus was saying. Every time he used the phrase "Son of Man," he crowned himself. Would a decent fellow walk around making such a claim? You want a guy like this in your neighborhood?

And what about his "I Am" statements? "I am the light of the world." "I am the bread of life," "the resurrection and the life," and "the way, the truth, and the life." And most stunning, "Before Abraham was born, I am!"[10]

By claiming the "I Am" title, Jesus was equating himself with God.

Jesus claimed to be able to forgive sins — a privilege only God can exercise (Matthew 9:4 – 7). He claimed to be greater than Jonah, Solomon, Jacob, and even Abraham (Matthew 12:38 – 42; John 4:12 – 14; 8:53 – 56). Jesus said that John the Baptist was the greatest man who had ever lived but implied that he was greater (Matthew 11:11). Jesus commanded people to pray in his name (John 14:13 – 14). He claimed to be greater than the temple (Matthew 12:6), greater than the Sabbath (Matthew 12:8). He claimed his words would outlive heaven and earth (Mark 13:31) and that all authority in heaven and on earth had been given to him (Matthew 28:18–20).

Does a decent fellow say things like this? No, but a demented fool does.

Maybe Jesus was a megalomaniac on par with Alexander the Great or Adolf Hitler. But, honestly, could a madman do what Jesus did?

Look at the devotion he inspired. People didn't just respect Jesus. They liked him; they left their homes and businesses and followed him. Men and women alike tethered their hope to his life. Impulsive people like Peter. Visionaries like Philip. Passionate men like John, careful men like Thomas, methodical men like Matthew the tax collector. When the men had left Jesus in the grave, it was the women who came to honor him — women from all walks of life, homemaking to philanthropy.

And people were better because of him. Madmen sire madmen: Saddam Hussein created murderers, Joseph Stalin created power addicts, Charles Manson created wackos. But Jesus transformed common dockworkers and net casters into the authors of history's greatest book and founders of its greatest movement. "They stand like a row of noble pillars towering far across the flats of time. But the sunlight that shines on them, and makes them visible, comes entirely from Him. He gave them all their greatness; and theirs is one of the most striking evidences of His."[11]

And what about his teaching? What about the day when Jesus' enemies sent officers to arrest him? Because of the crowd, they couldn't reach him directly. As they were pushing through the people, the officers were so gripped by his words that they abandoned their assignment. Their hearts were arrested, and Jesus was not. They returned to their superiors without a prisoner. Their defense? "No man ever spoke like this Man!" (John 7:46 NKJV).

Christ stunned people with his authority and clarity. His was not the mind of a deranged wild man. Demented fool? No. Deceiving fraud? Some have said so.

Some believe that Jesus masterminded the greatest scheme in the history of humanity, that he out-Ponzied the swindlers and out-hustled the hucksters. If that were true, billions of humans have been fleeced into following a first-century pied piper over the edge of a cliff.

Should we crown Christ as the foremost fraud in the world?

Not too quickly. Look at the miracles Jesus performed. The four gospels detail approximately thirty-six miracles and reference many more. He multiplied bread and fish, changed water into wine, calmed more than one storm, restored sight to more than one blind man. He healed contagious skin diseases, gave steps to the lame, purged demons, stopped a hemorrhage, even replaced a severed ear.

Yet, in doing so, Jesus never grandstanded his miraculous powers. Never went for fame or profit. Jesus performed miracles for two reasons: to prove his identity and to help his people.

Around AD 120, a man named Quadratus wrote the emperor Hadrian, defending Christianity. His apologetic included this sentence: "The works of our Saviour were lasting, for they were genuine: those who were healed and those who were raised from the dead were seen ... not merely while the Saviour was on earth, but also after his death; they were alive for quite a while, so that some of them lived even to our day."[12]

Had Jesus been a fraud or trickster, the Jerusalem congregation would have died a stillborn death. People would have denounced the miracles of Christ. But they did just the opposite. Can you imagine the apostles inviting testimonies? "If you were a part of the crowd he fed, one of the dead he raised, or one of the sick he healed, speak up and tell your story."

And speak they did. The church exploded like a fire on a West Texas prairie. Why? Because Jesus performed public, memorable miracles. He healed people.

And he loved people. He paid no heed to class or nationality, past sins or present accomplishments. The neediest and loneliest found a friend in Jesus:

- a woman scarcely clothed because of last night's affair. Christ befriended and defended her. (John 8:3–11)

- an unscrupulous tax collector left friendless because of his misdealings. Christ became his mentor. (Luke 19:2–10)

- a multiple divorcée who drew from the well in the heat of the day to avoid the stares of the villagers. Jesus gave her his attention. (John 4:5–26)

Could a lying sham love this way? If his intent was to trick people out of their money or worship, he did a pitifully poor job, for he died utterly broke and virtually abandoned.

What if Peter was correct? "You are the Messiah" (Mark 8:29).

What if Jesus really was, and is, the Son of God? If so, then we can relish this wonderful truth: we never travel alone. True, we cannot see the runway. We do not know what the future holds. But, no, we are not alone.

We have what Jim O'Neill had: the commander's voice to guide us home. Let's heed it, shall we? Let's issue the necessary Mayday prayer and follow the guidance that God sends. If so, we will hear what O'Neill heard.

BBC News made the recording of the final four minutes of the flight available. Listen and you'll hear the patient voice of a confident commander. "You've missed the runway this time ... Let's start another gentle right-hand turn ... Keep the right turn coming .... Roll out left ... No need to worry ... Roll out left. Left again, left again ... Keep coming down ... Turn left, turn left ... Hey, no problem ... Can you see the runway now?... So you cannot see the runway?... Keep coming down ..."

And then finally, "You are safe to land."[13]

I'm looking forward to hearing that final sentence someday. Aren't you?

Nick, 17 — Trusting God's voice gives me strength and courage. I've made mistakes and learned to trust God. Wise people you can't always trust, [but] God is the Almighty; he will answer your call when you need him. The Bible is the truth. It helps guide you through life and other obstacles. Trusting God has made a difference in me.

DON'T JUST SIT THERE . . .

Thank God that Jesus is completely trustworthy; ask him to help you to grow to trust in Jesus more and more.

Make a quick list of the three most trustworthy people in your life. Circle the one who has the most in common with Jesus.

Ask a good friend to describe to you whom they believe Jesus to be. Be prepared to answer the question yourself.

Pay attention to the next story you read or see and notice whom the hero is asked to trust in (e.g., the "force," himself or herself, a mentor, a system, etc.).

If you consider Jesus trustworthy, make a list of three things he has asked you to do. Circle any that you are not doing and write down why.

The next time you sing praise songs or hymns, pay attention to what they say about trusting God.

CHAPTER 5

WHEN GOD'S STORY
BECOMES YOURS ...

YOU WON'T BE
FORSAKEN

THINK ABOUT IT!

For a while there, it seemed like the only stories anyone was telling were vampire stories. A flood of books, TV shows, movies, and video games wanted to introduce us to their dark and brooding antiheroes, their "good vampires."

We like these kinds of characters because they're complicated. They've done a lot of bad things, but they want to do better. They agonize over their guilt and try to make up for it with heroic acts of self-sacrifice. Maybe you can relate to that impulse. Everyone can work up a good guilt over some terrible thing they've done, and guilt is motivating for a while.

But you are not a vampire. When you enter into God's story through faith in Jesus, all those sins stop being yours. He suffered and died for them so you don't have to. You might still feel the temptation, but your mission isn't to make up for your crimes. It's to accomplish God's mission for you as a brand-new creature.

Tennessee gives drunk drivers a new wardrobe. The Volunteer State has a special gift for any person convicted of driving their streets under the influence of alcohol. A blaze orange vest. Offenders are required to wear it in public three different days for eight hours at a time while picking up litter from the side of the highway. Stenciled on the back in four-inch-tall letters are the words "I AM A DRUNK DRIVER."[14]

No doubt they deserve the punishment. In fact, given the threat they've imposed upon the highways, they deserve three days of public humiliation. I don't question the strategy of the state.

But I wonder why we do the same to ourselves. Why we dress ourselves in our mistakes, don the robe of poor choices. Don't we? We step into our closets and sort through our regrets and rebellion and, for some odd reason, vest up.

I DISAPPOINTED MY PARENTS.

I HAVE IMPURE THOUGHTS.

I MAKE BAD CHOICES.

Sometimes we cover the vest with a blouse or blazer of good behavior. Mrs. Adams did. She's not the only person who ever came to see me while wearing a vest, but she was the first. I was only days into my first full-time church position in Miami, Florida. I'd barely unpacked my books when the receptionist asked if I could receive a visitor.

The senior minister was occupied, and I was next in line. I stepped into the conference room, where she sat stirring a cup of coffee. She was a slight woman, wearing a nice dress and carrying a designer purse. She looked at me for only a moment, then back at the cup. That I was several years her junior didn't seem to matter.

"I left my family," she blurted. No greeting, introduction, or small talk. Just a confession.

I took a seat and asked her to tell me about it. I didn't have to ask twice. Too much pressure, temptation, and stress. So she walked out on her kids — ten years before she came to see me! What struck me about her story was not what she had done but how long she'd been living with her guilt. A decade! And now, hungry for help, she had a request.

"Can you give me some work to do?"

"What? Do you need some money?"

She looked at me like I was a doctor unacquainted with penicillin. "No, I need some work. Anything. Letters to file, floors to sweep. Give me some work to do. I'll feel better if I do some work for God."

Welcome to the vest system. Hard to hide it. Harder still to discard it. But we work at doing so. Emphasis on the word *work*. Overcome bad deeds with good ones. Offset bad choices with godly ones, stupid moves with righteous ones. But the vest-removal process is flawed. No one knows what work to do or how long to do it. Shouldn't the Bible, of all books, tell us? But it doesn't. Instead, the Bible tells us how God's story redeems our story.

Jesus' death on the cross is not a secondary theme in Scripture; it is the core. The English word *crucial* comes from the Latin for cross (*crux*). The crucial accomplishment of Christ occurred on the cross. Lest we miss the message, God encased the climax of his story in high drama.

The garden: Jesus crying out, the disciples running out, the soldiers bursting in.

The trials: early morning mockery and deceit. Jews scoffing. Pilate washing.

The soldiers: weaving thorns, slashing whips, pounding nails.

Jesus: bloodied, beaten. More crimson than clean. Every sinew afire with pain.

And God: He ebonized the sky and shook the earth. He cleaved the rocks and ripped the temple curtain. He untombed the entombed and unveiled the Holy of Holies in the temple.

But first he heard the cry of his Son.

"My God, my God, why have you forsaken me?" (Matthew 27:46).

Forsaken. Visceral, painful. The word reminds us of abandonment, of desertion, of being left helpless, alone, cast out, of being completely forgotten.

Jesus forsaken? Does Scripture not declare, "I have not seen the righteous forsaken," and assure that "the LORD ... does not forsake His saints" (Psalm 37:25, 28 NKJV)?

Indeed it does. But in that hour Jesus was anything but righteous. This was the moment in which "God put the wrong on him who never did anything wrong" (2 Corinthians 5:21 MSG). "GOD ... piled all our sins, everything we've done wrong, on him, on him. He was beaten, he was tortured, but he didn't say a word" (Isaiah 53:6–7 MSG).

He dressed Christ in vests. Our vests, each and every one.

I BETRAYED MY FRIENDS.

I LIED TO MY TEACHER.

I HURT MYSELF TO FEEL GOOD.

I CURSED MY GOD.

As if Jesus deserved them, he wore them. Our sins, our vests, were put on Christ. "The LORD has laid on him the iniquity of us all" (Isaiah 53:6). "He bore the sin of many" (Isaiah 52:12). Paul proclaimed that God made Christ "to be sin"· (2 Corinthians 5:21) and become "a curse for us" (Galatians 3:13). Peter agreed: "'[Jesus] bore our sins' in his body on the cross" (1 Peter 2:24).

This is the monumental offer of God. What does God say to the woman who wants to work and offset her guilt? Simple: the work has been done. My Son wore your sin on himself, and I punished it there.

"For Christ also suffered once for sins, the just for the unjust, that He might bring us to God" (1 Peter 3:18 NKJV).

On August 16, 1987, Northwest Airlines flight 225 crashed after taking off from the Detroit airport, killing 155 people. The lone survivor was four-year-old Cecelia from Tempe, Arizona. Rescuers found her in such good condition that they wondered if she'd actually been on the flight. Perhaps she was riding in one of the cars into which the airplane crashed. But, no, her name was on the manifest.

While the exact nature of events may never be known, Cecelia's survival may have been due to her mother's quick response. Initial reports from the scene indicate that, as the plane was falling, her mother, Paula Cichan, unbuckled her own seat belt, got down on her knees in front of her daughter, and wrapped her arms and body around the girl. She separated her from the force of the fall ... and the daughter survived.[15]

God did the same for us. He wrapped himself around us and felt the full force of the fall. He took the unrelaxed punishment of the guilty. He died, not like a sinner, but as a sinner — in our place. "By a wonderful exchange our sins are now not ours but Christ's, and Christ's righteousness is not Christ's but ours."[16] His sacrifice is a sufficient one. Our accomplishments don't enhance it. Our stumbles don't diminish it. The sacrifice of Christ is a total and unceasing and accomplished work.

"It is finished," Jesus announced (John 19:30). His prayer of abandonment is followed by a cry of accomplishment. Not "It is begun" or "It is initiated" or "It is a work in progress." No, "It is finished."

You can remove your vest. Toss the thing in a trash barrel and set it on fire. You need never wear it again. Does better news exist? Actually, yes. There is more. We not only remove our vest—we don his! He is "our righteousness" (1 Corinthians 1:30).

Baxter, 15—As teenagers we walk around with guilt, pain, or feelings of imperfection. Some carry more than others, but most of us have something we constantly regret. Only through Jesus Christ can we find our true happiness and contentedness with ourselves. It says in Philippians that I can do all things through Christ who strengthens me. In reading this I know that no matter what my choices and decisions, I can overcome anything through the Lord Jesus Christ. We just have to know that no matter what we have done or not done, Jesus died on the cross for us and our sins. So we don't have to wear our vests of imperfection, because in Jesus we are complete.

God does not simply remove our failures; he dresses us in the goodness of Christ! "For all of you who were baptized into Christ have clothed yourselves with Christ" (Galatians 3:27).

Think about this for a moment. When you make God's story yours, he covers you in Christ. You wear him like a vest. Old labels no longer apply — only labels that would be appropriately worn by Jesus Christ. Can you think of a few phrases for your new vest? How about

- royal priest (1 Peter 2:9)

- complete (Colossians 2:10 NKJV)

- free from condemnation (Romans 8:1)

- secure (John 10:28)

- established and anointed one
  (2 Corinthians 1:21 NKJV)

- God's coworker (2 Corinthians 6:1)

- God's temple (1 Corinthians 3:16 – 17)

- God's workmanship (Ephesians 2:10 NKJV)

How do you like that outfit?

"Now you're dressed in a new wardrobe. Every item of your new way of life is custom-made by the Creator, with his label on it. All the old fashions are now obsolete" (Colossians 3:10 MSG). Don't mess with the old clothes any longer. "As far as the east is from the west, so far has he removed our transgressions from us" (Psalm 103:12).

How far is the east from the west? Farther and farther by the moment. Travel west and you can make laps around the globe and never go east. Journey east and, if you desire, maintain an easterly course indefinitely. Not so with the other two directions. If you go north or south, you'll eventually reach the North or South Pole and change directions. But east and west have no turning points.

Neither does God. When he sends your sins to the east and you to the west, you can be sure of this: he doesn't see you in your sins. His forgiveness is irreversible. "He does not treat us as our sins deserve or repay us according to our iniquities" (Psalm 103:10).

Headline this truth: when God sees you, he sees his Son, not your sin. God "blots out your transgressions" and "remembers your sins no more" (Isaiah 43:25). No probation. No exception. No reversals.

He did his due diligence. He saw your secret deeds and heard your unsaid thoughts. The lies, the lusts, the longings — he knows them all. God assessed your life from first day to last, from worst moment to best, and made his decision.

"I want that child in my kingdom."

You cannot convince him otherwise.

Look on his city gates for proof. In the last pages of the Bible, John describes the entrance to the New Jerusalem:

She had a great and high wall with twelve gates ...
and names written on them, which are the names of
the twelve tribes of the children of Israel. ...

Now the wall of the city had twelve foundations,
and on them were the names of the twelve apostles
of the Lamb.

—REVELATION 21:12, 14 NKJV

God engraved the names of the sons of Jacob on his
gateposts. More ragamuffins than reverends. Their rap
sheets include stories of mass murder (Genesis 34), incest
(Genesis 38:13 – 18), and brotherly betrayal (Genesis
37:17 – 28). They behaved more like lowbrow reality stars
than a wholesome TV family. Yet God carved their names
on the New Jerusalem gates.

And dare we mention the names on the foundations?
Peter, the apostle who saved his own skin instead of his
Savior's. James and John, who jockeyed for VIP seats in
heaven. Thomas, the dubious, who insisted on a personal
audience with the resurrected Jesus. These were the disciples who told the children to leave Jesus alone (Luke
18:15), who told Jesus to leave the hungry on their own
(Matthew 14:15), and who chose to leave Jesus alone to
face his crucifixion (Matthew 26:36 – 45). Yet all of their

names appear on the foundations. Matthew's does. Peter's does. Bartholomew's does.

And yours? It's not engraved in the gate, but it is written in the Book of the Lamb. Not in pencil marks that can be erased, but with blood that will not be removed. No need to keep God happy; he is satisfied. No need to pay the price; Jesus paid it.

All.

Lose your old vest. You look better wearing his.

DON'T JUST SIT THERE ...

Thank God that Jesus paid the penalty for all of your sins once and for all on the cross. Ask him to help you to believe that so much that you don't try to take them back.

This week, notice any stories that are built on the idea of someone trying to make up for something wrong they've done by doing something good. Think about why that can never work in real life for Christians.

Ask a friend who may or may not be a Christian if they believe we can "pay off" our evil choices by doing enough good. Be ready to tell them what you think about that (after reading this chapter).

Make a quick list (in your head, maybe) of the three worst things you ever remember doing. Put an X through the ones that Jesus completely paid for on the cross; circle any that you think are too bad for God to forgive. Then put an X though those too.

Make your Facebook, Twitter, or other social network status Romans 8:1 for a whole day.

CHAPTER 6

WHEN GOD'S STORY
BECOMES YOURS ...

YOUR
FINAL CHAPTER
BECOMES
A PREFACE

THINK ABOUT IT!

Do you remember that old movie *The Princess Bride*? If you've never seen it, watch it soon. It's an awesome story that's really about telling awesome stories. It ends the way all the best stories do: "And they all lived happily ever after."

Modern storytellers work hard to keep their stories from ending so neatly. "Real life is messy," they say. "People won't buy it if everything turns out exactly right in the end. It won't ring true. It will feel like some kind of fairy tale."

But while some of us appreciate a good, dark story that reflects our messy world, most people also love stories with happy, feel-good endings. We want to believe everything will come together and everyone will be okay. And that is exactly the ending God promises to those who live their story inside of his by trusting in Jesus.

Are you expecting to live happily ever after ... after this life is over?

CARL McCUNN, AN AFFABLE TEXAN WITH A LOVE OF THE outdoors, moved to Alaska in the late 1970s. He took a trucking job on the Trans-Alaska Pipeline, where he made good money, fast friends, and concocted an adventure that still stirs bewilderment in the forty-ninth state.

At the age of thirty-five, he embarked on a five-month photography expedition in the wild. Friends describe how seriously he prepared for the quest, devoting a year to plan making and detail checking. He solicited advice and purchased supplies. And then, in March 1981, he hired a bush pilot to drop him at a remote lake near the Coleen River, some seventy miles northeast of Fort Yukon. He took two rifles, a shotgun, fourteen hundred pounds of provisions, and five hundred rolls of film.

He set up his tent and set about his season of isolation, blissfully unaware of an overlooked detail that would cost him his life.

He had made no arrangement to be picked up.

His unbelievable blunder didn't dawn on him until August. We know this because of a hundred-page loose-leaf diary the Alaska state troopers found near his body the following February. In an understatement the size of Mount McKinley, McCunn wrote: "I think I should have used more foresight about arranging my departure."

As the days shortened and air chilled, he began searching the ground for food and the skies for rescue. He was running low on ammunition. Hiking out was impossible. He had no solution but to hope someone in the city would notice his absence.

By the end of September, the snow was piling, the lake was frozen, and supplies were nearly gone. His body fat began to metabolize, making it more difficult to stay warm. Temperatures hovered around zero, and frostbite began to attack his fingers and toes.

By late November, McCunn was out of food, strength, and optimism. One of his final diary entries reads, "This is sure a slow and agonizing way to die."[17]

Isolated with no rescue. Trapped with no exit. Nothing to do but wait for the end. Chilling.

And puzzling. Why no exit strategy? Didn't he know that every trip comes to an end? It's not like his excursion would last forever.

Ours won't.

This heart will feel a final pulse. These lungs will empty a final breath. The hand that directs this pen across the page will fall limp and still. Barring the return of Christ, I will die. So will you. "Death is the most democratic institution on earth.... It allows no discrimination, tolerates no exceptions. The mortality rate of mankind is the same the world over: one death per person."[18]

Or, as the psalmist asked, "Who can live and not see death, or who can escape the power of the grave?" (Psalm 89:48). Young and old, good and bad, rich and poor. Neither gender is spared; no class is exempt. "No one has power over the time of their death" (Ecclesiastes 8:8).

The genius, the rich, the poor—no one outruns it or outsmarts it. Princess Diana died. Michael Jackson died. John Kennedy died. We all die. Nearly 2 people a second, more than 6,000 an hour, more than 155,000 every day, about 57 million a year.[19] We don't escape death.

The finest surgeon might enhance your life but can't eliminate your death. The Hebrew writer was blunt: "People are destined to die once" (Hebrews 9:27). Exercise all you want. Eat nothing but health food, and pop fistfuls of vitamins. Stay out of the sun, away from alcohol, and off drugs. Do your best to stay alive, and still, you die.

Death seems like such a dead end.

Until we read Jesus' resurrection story.

"He is not here. He has risen from the dead as he said he would" (Matthew 28:6 NCV).

It was Sunday morning after the Friday execution. Jesus' final breath had sucked the air out of the universe. As his body seemed to be a-moldering in the grave, no one was placing bets on a resurrection.

His enemies were satisfied with their work. The spear to his side guaranteed his death. His tongue was silenced. His last deed done. They raised a toast to a dead Jesus. Their only concern was those pesky disciples. The religious leaders made this request of Pilate: "So give the order for the tomb to be made secure until the third day. Otherwise, his disciples may come and steal the body and tell the people that he has been raised from the dead" (Matthew 27:64).

No concern was necessary. The disciples were at meltdown. When Jesus was arrested, "all the disciples forsook Him and fled" (Matthew 26:56 NKJV). Peter followed from a distance but caved in and cursed Christ. John watched Jesus die, but we have no record that John gave any thought to ever seeing him again. The other followers didn't even linger; they cowered in Jerusalem's cupboards and corners for fear of the cross that bore their names.

No one dreamed of a Sunday morning miracle. Peter didn't ask John, "What will you say when you see Jesus?" Mary didn't ponder, *How will he appear?* They didn't encourage each other with quotes of his promised return. They could have. At least four times Jesus had said words like these: "The Son of Man is being betrayed into the hands of men, and they will kill Him. And after He is killed, He will rise the third day."[20] You'd think someone would mention this prophecy and do the math. "Hmm, he died yesterday. Today is the second day. He promised to rise on the third day. Tomorrow is the third day ... Friends, I think we'd better wake up early tomorrow."

But Saturday saw no such plans. On Saturday the Enemy had won, courage was gone, and hope caught the last train to the coast. They planned to embalm Jesus, not talk to him.

When the Sabbath was over, Mary Magdalene, Mary the mother of James, and Salome bought spices so that they might go to anoint Jesus' body. Very early on the first day of the week, just after sunrise, they were on their way to the tomb and they asked each other, "Who will roll the stone away from the entrance of the tomb?"

—MARK 16:1–3

Easter parade? Victory march? Hardly. More like a funeral procession. It may have been Sunday morning, but their world was stuck on Saturday.

It was left to the angel to lead them into Sunday.

There was a violent earthquake, for an angel of the Lord came down from heaven and, going to the tomb, rolled back the stone and sat on it. His appearance was like lightning, and his clothes were white as snow. The guards were so afraid of him that they shook and became like dead men.

The angel said to the women, "Do not be afraid, for I know that you are looking for Jesus, who was crucified. He is not here; he has risen, just as he said. Come and see the place where he lay."

—MATTHEW 28:2–6

God shook up the cemetery. Trees swayed, and the ground trembled. Pebbles bounced, and the women struggled to maintain their balance. They looked in the direction of the tomb only to see the guards—scared stiff, paralyzed, and sprawled on the ground. Hard to miss the irony: the guards of the dead appear dead, while the dead one appears to be living. Take that, Devil. Remember the famous play on Nietzsche's statement?[21]

"GOD is DEAD!"

Nietzsche.

"NIETZSCHE is DEAD!"

God.

The angel sat on the dislodged tombstone. He did not stand in defiance or crouch in alertness. He sat. Legs crossed and whistling? In my imagination at least. The angel sat upon the *stone*. Again, the irony. The very rock intended to mark the resting place of a dead Christ became the resting place of his living angel. And then the announcement.

"He has risen."

Three words in English. Just one in Greek, the language of the New Testament. *Çgerthç*. So much rests on the validity of this one word. If it is false, then the whole of Christianity collapses like a poorly told joke. Yet, if it is true, then God's story has turned your final chapter into a preface. If the angel was correct, then you can believe this: Jesus descended into the coldest cell of death's prison and allowed the warden to lock the door and smelt the keys in a furnace. And just when the demons began to dance and prance, Jesus pressed pierced hands against the inner walls of the cavern. From deep within he shook the cemetery. The ground rumbled, and the tombstones tumbled.

And out he marched, the cadaver turned king, with the mask of death in one hand and the keys of heaven in the other. *Çgerthç!* He has risen!

Not risen from sleep. Not risen from confusion. Not risen from stupor or slumber. Not spiritually raised from the dead; *physically* raised. The women and disciples didn't see a phantom or experience a sentiment. They saw Jesus in the flesh. "It is I myself!" he assured them (Luke 24:39).

The Emmaus-bound disciples thought Jesus was a fellow pilgrim. His feet touched the ground. His hands touched the bread he was serving. Mary mistook him for a gardener. Thomas touched his wounds. The disciples ate fish that he cooked. The resurrected Christ did physical deeds in a physical body. "I am not a ghost," he explained (Luke 24:39 NLT). "Handle Me and see, for a spirit does not have flesh and bones as you see I have" (verse 39 NKJV).

The bodily resurrection means everything. If Jesus lives on only in spirit and deeds, he is but one of a thousand dead heroes. But if he lives on in flesh and bone, he is the King who pressed his heel against the head of death. What he did with his own grave he promises to do with your coffin: empty it.

A curious thing happened as I was rewriting this chapter. While reading the above paragraph, I heard my computer signal an email arrival. I stopped to read it. A friend had just returned from the funeral of his ninety-six-year-old aunt, and he wanted to tell me about it.

> Max,
>
> Until about a year ago, you couldn't keep up with my Aunt Wanda. Seriously—she had such energy you just couldn't believe it. Her eyesight was failing so completely that her energy almost made it dangerous to go unfamiliar places with her. Her eyes couldn't see the crack in the sidewalk that she was about to trot over at ninety miles an hour!!!
>
> About a year ago she started having difficulty breathing. The doctor found a mass in her chest that was almost certainly cancer. But at ninety-five there was little reason to do surgery—even exploratory. The better plan was to keep her comfortable.
>
> It was only in the last three days of her life that the mass became painful to the point she needed medication to fight the pain. The pain became so severe so quickly

that she was given enough morphine to sedate her and basically keep her in an unconscious state.

But as she began to pass from this world into the next, her sight became clear, she was released of the pain, and even in her unconscious state, she began to have conversations with those that had gone before her. She saw her mother (who was her best friend) and talked to her. And, my favorite part, she saw my dad and their brother.

My dad and their brother (Uncle Marvin) were constantly playing practical jokes on their sister (Aunt Wanda). She always referred to them as "the boys" or "those boys." I have no idea what they did or how they greeted her at heaven's door, but whatever it was made her laugh so hard that she literally pulled her legs up to her chest and doubled over laughing. "I can't believe you boys! Oh my goodness . . . you boys!" She literally took her last breaths laughing. I can't wait to find out what she saw. But she saw something grand![22]

You will too.

Will you die laughing? I don't know. But die in peace, for certain. Death is not the final chapter in your story. In death you will step into the arms of the One who declared, "I am the resurrection and the life. The one who believes in me will live, even though they die; and whoever lives by believing in me will never die" (John 11:25 – 26).

Winston Churchill believed this. The British prime minister planned his own funeral. According to his instructions, two buglers were positioned high in the dome of St. Paul's Cathedral. At the conclusion of the service, the first one played taps, the signal of a day completed. Immediately thereafter, with the sounds of the first song still ringing in the air, the second bugler played reveille, the song of a day begun.[23]

Appropriate song. Death is no pit but a passageway; not a crisis but a corner turn. Dominion of the grim reaper? No. Territory of the Soul Keeper, who will someday announce, "Your dead will live, your corpses will get to their feet. All you dead and buried, wake up! Sing! Your dew is morning dew catching the first rays of sun, the earth bursting with life, giving birth to the dead" (Isaiah 26:19 MSG).

Play on, bugler. Play on.

Danielle—Even though death can be a wonderful thing
and an absolute celebration, it is most certainly a loss. It's sad,
painful, and it's just not fair. When I think about death, I just
cringe at the thought of it because I think about the people I love
leaving me. I can't imagine going through life without them. But
then I think about Jesus. And the love God has for me. And my
heart just melts. It is so comforting that those who trust in Jesus
get to stay forever in a place like heaven. And even better, that
I'll get to see my Savior, the one who shed blood and suffered so
much for me. I'll get to see Jesus face-to-face! And that in itself
is all it takes to get me excited to go to heaven.

DON'T JUST SIT THERE . . .

Make a quick list of three stories in which the hero dies in the end. Circle your favorite one. Think about how the end of that story would feel different if the hero believed (or didn't) that he or she would immediately be in heaven with God.

If your parent is a Christian, ask them how life would be different if they didn't believe they would be resurrected to a new life after they died. How would they live if they didn't believe in an afterlife in heaven? Why?

Thank God that because Jesus was raised from the dead, you will be too.

Ask God to help you not to fear dying, but to look forward to living forever with him.

Ask a friend or two if they would take more or fewer risks in life if they believed differently about what would happen after they died.

Grab any book nearby; the bigger the better. Open it and hold the very first page between your thumb and finger. Think about the reality that this page represents your whole life on this side of heaven and the rest of the book represents just the beginning of the rest of your life, your real life, in eternity.

CHAPTER 7

WHEN GOD'S STORY
BECOMES YOURS ...

POWER
MOVES IN

THINK ABOUT IT!

It's the old Superman-versus-Batman debate. Superman fans want superpowers. The Man of Steel is cool because he is stronger, faster, and more powerful. Batman fans love that the guy doesn't have any powers; he's just smarter, more inventive, and more committed than the bad guys.

Whichever side you take in that debate, the story you are living through faith in Jesus is all about superpowers. In fact, one of the main points in the story is that you and I *cannot* be good enough on our own to overcome evil. We've already lost. We need to be bitten by that radioactive spider to have a shot at winning the battles we will face.

Check that. The Holy Spirit is not a spider, and he doesn't make you supernaturally strong so you can win your own battles. He makes you supernaturally strong so you can do everything the Storyteller has planned for your character. He empowers you to accomplish what he asks of you.

It is your destiny.

Sergio, 16—If I could choose a superpower, it would be to make wishes come true. I would use it to help people and make them happy. Help them be a normal person with capabilities. I would most like to help the homeless. I would also help those who need it, help them find God. So no matter what bad things may have happened in the past, we could all be happy to know how to live life.

WHAT GOT INTO PETER? SEVEN WEEKS AGO HE WAS HID-ing because of Jesus; today he is proclaiming the death of Jesus. Before the crucifixion, he denied Christ; now he announces Christ. On the eve of Good Friday, you couldn't get him to speak up. Today, you can't get him to shut up! "My fellow Jews, and all who are in Jerusalem, listen to me. Pay attention to what I have to say" (Acts 2:14 NCV).

What got into Peter?

He was a coward at the crucifixion. A kind coward but a coward nonetheless. A question from a servant girl undid him. A soldier didn't bludgeon him. The Sanhedrin didn't browbeat him. Rome didn't threaten to export him to Siberia. No, a waitress from the downtown diner heard his accent and said he knew Jesus. Peter panicked. He not only denied his Lord; he bleeped the very idea. "Then Peter began to place a curse on himself and swear, 'I don't know the man!'" (Matthew 26:74 NCV).

But look at him on the day of Pentecost, declaring to a throng of thousands, "God has made this Jesus — the man you nailed to the cross — both Lord and Christ" (Acts 2:36 NCV). Gutsy language. Lynch mobs feed on these accusations. The same crowd that shouted, "Crucify him!" could crucify him.

From wimp to warrior in fifty days. What happened?

Oh, how we need to know. We admire the Pentecost Peter yet identify with the Passover one. We battle addictions we can't shake, pasts we can't escape, bills we can't pay, sorrow that won't fade.

Our convictions wrinkle, and resolve melts. And we

wonder why. We look at other believers and ask, Why is her life so fruitful and mine so barren? Why is his life so powerful and mine so weak? Aren't we saved by the same Christ? Don't we read the same Scripture and rally around the same cross? Why do some look like the early Peter and others like the latter? Or, better question, why do I vacillate between the two in any given week?

Jesus embedded an answer in his final earthly message. He told Peter and the other followers, "Wait here to receive the promise from the Father which I told you about. John baptized people with water, but in a few days you will be baptized with the Holy Spirit" (Acts 1:4 – 5 NCV).

What got into Peter?

God's Spirit did. Ten days after Jesus' ascension into heaven, "all of them were filled with the Holy Spirit" (Acts 2:4). The followers experienced a gushing forth, a tremendous profusion. They were drenched in power. They all were "sons and daughters ... young men ... old men ... servants, both men and women" (Acts 2:17 – 18). The Holy Spirit, in his own time and according to his own way, filled the followers with supernatural strength.

Didn't Jesus promise this event? As his days on earth came to an end, he said, "But very truly I tell you, it is for your good that I am going away. Unless I go away, the

Advocate will not come to you; but if I go, I will send him to you" (John 16:7).

The bad news: Jesus was going away. The wonderful news: Jesus was sending them the Spirit. During his earthly ministry Jesus lived near the disciples. The Holy Spirit, however, would live *in* the disciples. What Jesus did with the followers, the Spirit would do through them and us. Jesus healed; the Spirit heals through us. Jesus taught; the Spirit teaches through us. Jesus comforted; the Spirit comforts through us. The Spirit continues the work of Christ.

The Holy Spirit is not enthusiasm, compassion, or bravado. He might stimulate such emotions, but he himself is a person. He determines itineraries (Acts 16:6), distributes spiritual gifts (1 Corinthians 12:7 – 11), and selects church leaders (Acts 13:2). He teaches (John 14:26), guides (John 16:13), and comforts (John 16:7 KJV).

"He dwells with you and will be in you" (John 14:17 NKJV). Occasional guest? No sir. The Holy Spirit is a year-round resident in the hearts of those who believe. As God's story becomes our story, his power becomes our power. Then why do we suffer from power failures?

I believe we make the mistake the Welsh woman made. She lived many years ago in a remote valley but determined that it would be worth the cost and trouble to have electricity in her home. Several weeks after the installation, the power company noticed that she had barely used any. So they sent a meter reader to see what was wrong.

"Is there a problem?" he asked.

"No," she answered, "we're quite satisfied. Every night we turn on the electric lights to see how to light our lamps."[24]

We're prone to do likewise: depend on God's Spirit to save us but not sustain us. We are like the Galatians whom Paul asked, "After beginning by means of the Spirit, are you now trying to finish by means of the flesh?" (Galatians 3:3). We turn to him to get us started, and then continue in our own strength.

The Christians in Ephesus did this. The apostle Paul assured them that they had received the Spirit. God "put his special mark of ownership on you by giving you the Holy Spirit that he had promised" (Ephesians 1:13 NCV). Even so, he had to urge them to be "filled with the Spirit" (Ephesians 5:18). Interesting. Can a person be saved and not full of the Holy Spirit? They were in Ephesus.

And in Jerusalem. When the apostles instructed the church to select deacons, they said, "So, brothers and sisters, choose seven of your own men who are good, full of the Spirit and full of wisdom" (Acts 6:3 NCV). The fact that men "full of the Spirit" were to be chosen suggests that men lacking in the Spirit were present. We can have the Spirit but not let the Spirit of God have us.

> **Christian, 17** — Living independently of others is something I often feel the need to prove. I shrug off help from my friends, parents, and worst of all, God. I've come to realize that living my life in a Christian manner without him in my life is impossible. If I am going to live independently from the world, I must be dependent on God.

When God's Spirit directs us, we actually "keep in step with the Spirit" (Galatians 5:25). He is the drum major; we are the marching band. He is the sergeant; we are the platoon. He directs and leads; we obey and follow. Not always that easy, is it? We tend to go our own way.

Some time ago I purchased a new cartridge for my computer printer. But when I used it, no letters appeared on the page. It was half an hour before I noticed the thin strip of tape covering the outlet of the cartridge. There was plenty of ink, but until the tape was removed, no impression could be made.

Is there anything in your life that needs to be removed? Any impediment to the impression of God's Spirit? We can grieve the Spirit with our angry words (Ephesians

4:29 – 30; Isaiah 63:10) and resist the Spirit in our disobedience (Acts 7:51). We can test or conspire against the Spirit in our plottings (Acts 5:9). We can even quench the Spirit by having no regard for God's teachings. "Never damp the fire of the Spirit, and never despise what is spoken in the name of the Lord" (1 Thessalonians 5:19 – 20 Phillips).

Here is something that helps me stay in step with the Spirit. We know that "the fruit of the Spirit is love, joy, peace, patience, kindness, goodness, faithfulness, gentleness, self-control" (Galatians 5:22 – 23 NASB). God's Spirit creates and distributes these characteristics. They are indicators on my spiritual dashboard. So, whenever I sense them, I know I am walking in the Spirit. Whenever I lack them, I know I am out of step with the Spirit.

I sensed his corrective pull just yesterday at a Sunday service. A dear woman stopped me as I was entering the church building. She didn't agree with a comment I had made in a sermon the week before and wanted to express her opinion ... in the foyer ... in a loud voice ... ten minutes prior to the service.

What's more, she pressed the nerve of my pet peeve. "Other people feel the same way." Grrr. Who are these "other people"? How many "other people" are there? And why, for crying out loud, don't "other people" come and talk to me?

By now it was time for the service to begin. I was more in a mood to bear hunt than to preach. I couldn't get my mind off the woman and the "other people." I drove home from the morning service beneath a cloud. Rather than love, joy, peace, and patience, I felt anger, frustration, and impatience. I was completely out of step with the Spirit. And I had a choice. I could march to my own beat, or I could get back in rhythm. I knew what to do.

I made the phone call. "I didn't feel like we quite finished the conversation we began in the foyer," I told her. So we did. And over the next fifteen minutes, we discovered that our differences were based on a misunderstanding, and I learned that the "other people" consisted of her and her husband, and he was really okay.

To walk in the Spirit, respond to the promptings God gives you.

Don't sense any nudging? Just be patient and wait. Jesus told the disciples to "*wait* for the gift my Father promised ... the Holy Spirit" (Acts 1:4 – 5, emphasis mine). Abraham waited for the promised son. Moses waited forty years in the wilderness. Jesus waited thirty years before he began his ministry. God instills seasons of silence in his plan. Winter is needed for the soil to bear fruit. Time is needed for the development of a crop. And disciples wait for the move of God. Wait for him to move, nudge, and direct you. Somewhat as I'm learning to wait on my dance teacher.

My wife, Denalyn, and I are taking dance lessons. This was her announcement to me on our twenty-eighth wedding anniversary. She's been making such comments for years. "We need to learn to dance, honey." "What's there to learn?" was my stock reply, and I would remind her of the night we waltzed our way across the dance floor at my niece's wedding reception in 1985. She would mumble something about tractor-trailers having more finesse and drop the subject.

Of late she's been picking it back up. Now that our third little bird has winged her way out of our nest, it's time for the Mr. and Mrs. to slide their heels. So for my anniversary gift, she loaded me in the car, drove me to a shopping center, and parked in front of the Fred Astaire Dance Studio. (I know where they got the name. I just sat there and ... uh ... stared).

Our instructor is young enough to be our son. He wears a mustache-less beard and an innocent smile, and I wonder if he'd more quickly teach an elephant to pirouette than me to waltz. He spent the better part of the first class reminding me to "gently lead" my wife. "Place your hand beneath her shoulder blade and guide her."

He said I shoved and dragged her. Denalyn agreed. And, to convey his point, he danced with me. He matched one hand on mine, placed the other beneath my left shoulder blade, and off we went, *forward, forward, slide, slide,* following the beat of Barry Manilow across the room. I know, it's not a pretty sight. But it was a good lesson. I learned to follow his lead. He nudged me this way, led me that way, and, at the end I even did a nice twirl.

(Just kidding about the twirl. It was more of a tumble.)

It's nice to be led by a master. Won't you let your Master lead you?

> He guides the humble in what is right
> and teaches them his way.
>
> —PSALM 25:9

Whether you turn to the right or to the left, your ears will hear a voice behind you, saying, "This is the way; walk in it."

> —ISAIAH 30:21

Wait on the Spirit. If Peter and the apostles needed his help, don't we? They walked with Jesus for three years, heard his preaching, and saw his miracles. They saw the body of Christ buried in the grave and raised from the dead. They witnessed his upper room appearance and heard his instruction. Had they not received the best possible training? Weren't they ready?

Yet Jesus told them to wait on the Spirit. "Do not leave Jerusalem, but wait for the gift my Father promised … the Holy Spirit" (Acts 1:4–5).

Learn to wait, to be silent, to listen for his voice. Cherish stillness; sensitize yourself to his touch. "Just think — you don't need a thing, you've got it all! All God's gifts are right in front of you as you *wait expectantly* for our Master Jesus to arrive on the scene" (1 Corinthians 1:7–8 MSG, emphasis mine). You needn't hurry or scurry. The Spirit-led life does not panic; it trusts.

> God's power is very great for us who believe. That power is the same as the great strength God used to raise Christ from the dead and put him at his right side in the heavenly world.
>
> —EPHESIANS 1:19–20 NCV

The same hand that pushed the rock from the tomb can shove away your doubt. The same power that stirred the still heart of Christ can stir your flagging faith. The same strength that put Satan on his heels can, and will, defeat Satan in your life. Just keep the power supply open. Who knows, you may soon hear people asking, "What's gotten into you?"

DON'T JUST SIT THERE ...

Thank God that he does not just give you commands; he also gives you the power to obey him and do amazing things for his glory.

Ask God to give you the wisdom to know in what areas of your life you need to quit relying on your own strength and start relying on his power through the Spirit.

Read Galatians 5:22–23 and make a list of each of the fruits of the Holy Spirit in a Christian's life. Circle the ones you have noticed more of in your life in the last few years.

Look at that list again and think about one or two of the Christians you respect most. Draw a box around the ones in whose lives you have noticed growth.

One area of power the Holy Spirit gives us is the power to do something specific to serve other Christians in the church — but he doesn't give us power to do everything well. Pick one area of service in your church and jump into it. Notice if you feel "empowered" to do that thing or if it just feels like human work to you.

Write out Ephesians 1:17–19 on a piece of paper and pray it for yourself and one other Christian every day for a week.

CHAPTER 8

WHEN GOD'S STORY BECOMES YOURS ...

THE RIGHT DOORS OPEN

THINK ABOUT IT!

There's a great moment in the Lord of the Rings books where Sam talks about adventure stories. Everything seems to be going wrong for him and Frodo at that point. The plan has failed. Nothing is working. They can't imagine how they will ever accomplish the mission.

Sam delivers a great speech about how in the middle of the great stories full of darkness and danger you can't see any way the end could be happy. But still the heroes don't turn back. They keep going. And by the end, all the darkness is remembered as only a passing shadow.

In our stories, the ones we live inside of God's great story, we will come to moments like those, moments when we attempt great things and the way is blocked. We can't go through the door that seemed to be the answer to all the hard questions. But we must keep going another way, and trust that the Storyteller knows where he's taking us, that it's just a passing shadow.

I CAME HOME THE OTHER DAY TO A HOUSE OF BLOCKED doors. Not just shut doors, closed doors, or locked doors. Blocked doors.

Blame them on Molly, our nine-year-old, ninety-pound golden retriever, who, on most fronts, is a great dog. When it comes to kids and company, Molly sets a tail-wagging standard. But when it comes to doors, Molly just doesn't get it. Other dogs bark when they want out of the house; Molly scratches the door. She is the canine version of Freddy Krueger. Thanks to her, each of our doors has Molly marks.

We tried to teach her to bark, whine, or whistle; no luck. Molly thinks doors are meant to be clawed. So Denalyn came up with a solution: doggy doors. She installed Mollysized openings on two of our doors, and to teach Molly to use them, Denalyn blocked every other exit. She stacked furniture five feet deep and twice as wide. Molly got the message. She wasn't going out those doors.

And her feelings were hurt. I came home to find her with drooping ears and limp tail. She looked at the blocked door, then at us. "How could you do this to me?" her eyes pleaded. She walked from stack to stack. She didn't understand what was going on.

Maybe you don't either. You try one door after another, yet no one wants to be your friend. No university accepts your application. No doctor has a solution for your illness.

Obstacles pack your path. Road, barricaded. Doorway, padlocked. You, like Molly, walk from one blocked door to another. Do you know the frustration of a blocked door? If so, you have a friend in the apostle Paul.

Hannah, 17 — When applying to colleges this fall, I had my mind set on Texas A&M University. That had been my first choice and I waited four months for the acceptance letter. When it did arrive it wasn't what I'd hoped; I was not accepted. I was pretty devastated, but realized that it might truly be a blessing. I finally realized that maybe God needs me somewhere else; the door was closed but another door has opened for me.

He, Silas, and Timothy were on their second missionary journey. On his first one Paul enjoyed success at every stop. "They began to report all things that God had done with them and how He had opened a door of faith to the Gentiles" (Acts 14:27 NASB). God opened doors into Cyprus, Antioch, and Iconium. He opened the door of grace at the Jerusalem council and spurred spiritual growth in every city. "The churches were being strengthened in the faith, and were increasing in number daily" (Acts 16:5 NASB).

The missionaries felt the gusts at their backs, and then, all of a sudden, headwinds.

> Paul and his companions traveled throughout the region of Phrygia and Galatia, having been kept by the Holy Spirit from preaching the word in the province of Asia. When they came to the border of Mysia, they tried to enter Bithynia, but the Spirit of Jesus would not allow them to.
>
> —ACTS 16:6–7

Paul set his sights on Asia. Yet no doors opened. So the three turned north into Bithynia but encountered more blocked doors. They jiggled the knobs and pressed against the entrances but no access. We aren't told how or why God blocked the doors. Just that he did.

He still does.

God owns the key to every door. He is "opening doors no one can lock, locking doors no one can open" (Revelation 3:7 MSG). Once God closes a door, no one can open it. Once God shut the door of Noah's ark, only he could open it. Once he directed the soldiers to seal the tomb of Jesus, only he could open it. Once he blocks a door, we cannot open it. During a season of blocked doors, we, like Molly, can grow frustrated.

A few years ago, many of us at the church I pastor were convinced that our church needed a new sanctuary. We were bursting at the seams. Wouldn't God want us to build a larger auditorium? We thought so. We prayed for forty days, sought counsel from other churches. We weighed our options and designed a new facility. Sensing no divine reservation, we began the campaign.

All of a sudden the wind turned. In less than six months, construction costs increased 70 percent! Gulp. Still, we continued. We reduced the scope of the project and challenged the congregation to ante up more money. Even with their astounding generosity, we didn't raise enough money to build the sanctuary. I will never forget the weight I felt when I announced our decision not to build.

Didn't we pray? Didn't we seek God's will? Why would God close the door? Might it have something to do with this — the worst recession since the Great Depression looming less than a year away? God was protecting us. Moreover, within three months I would be diagnosed with a heart condition. God was protecting us.

It was a classic God's story/our story contrast. From our perspective we saw setbacks. God, however, saw an opportunity, an opportunity to keep us out of dangerous debt and bolster our leadership team with a new senior minister, Randy Frazee. A plan to protect us from a budget-busting mortgage and to grant us fresh leadership. God closed the wrong doors so he could lead us through the right one.

As God's story becomes yours, closed doors take on a new meaning. You no longer see them as interruptions of your plan but as indications of God's plan.

This is what Paul learned. God blocked his missionary team from going north, south, or east. Only west remained, so they ended up at Asia's westernmost point. They stood with their toes in the sand and looked out over the sea. As they slept, "Paul had a vision of a man of Macedonia standing and begging him, 'Come over to Macedonia and help us'" (Acts 16:9).

The closed doors in Asia led to an open-armed invitation to Europe. "Therefore, sailing from Troas, we ran a straight course to Samothrace, and the next day came to Neapolis, and from there to Philippi" (Acts 16:11–12 NKJV). They ran a "straight course." The wind was at their back. Blocked passages became full sails.

After several days Paul and his team went out of the city of Philippi to the riverside to attend a Jewish prayer service. While there, they met Lydia. "One of those listening was a woman from the city of Thyatira named Lydia, a dealer in purple cloth. She was a worshiper of God. The Lord opened her heart to respond to Paul's message" (Acts 16:14).

Read that verse too quickly, and you'll miss this account of the first convert in the West. Christianity was born in the East, and here the seeds of grace rode the winds of sovereignty over the Aegean Sea, fell on Grecian soil, and bore fruit in Philippi. Christ had his first European disciple ... and she was a she!

Is Lydia the reason the Holy Spirit blocked Paul's path? Was God ready to highlight the value of his daughters? Perhaps. In a culture that enslaved and degraded women, God elevated them to salvation coheirs with men. Proof?

The first person in the Western world to receive the Christian promise or host a Christian missionary was a female.

With her support Paul and his team got to work. Their efforts in Philippi were so effective that the pagan religious leaders were angered. They saw the people turning away from the temples and feared the loss of income. So they conjured up a story against Paul and Silas.

> Then the multitude rose up together against them; and the magistrates tore off their clothes and commanded them to be beaten with rods. And when they had laid many stripes on them, they threw them into prison, commanding the jailer to keep them securely. Having received such a charge, he put them into the inner prison and fastened their feet in the stocks.
>
> —ACTS 16:22–24 NKJV

Listen closely. Do you hear it? The old, familiar sound of keys turning and locks clicking. This time the doors swung closed on the hinges of a prison. Paul and Silas could have groaned, "Oh no, not again. Not another locked door."

But they didn't complain. From the bowels of the

prison emerged the most unexpected of sounds: praise and prayer. "About midnight Paul and Silas were praying and singing hymns to God, and the other prisoners were listening to them" (Acts 16:25).

Their feet were in stocks, yet their minds were in heaven. How could they sing at a time like this? The doors were slammed shut. Their feet were clamped. Backs ribboned with wounds. From whence came their song? There is only one answer: they trusted God and aligned their story to his.

> The ways of the LORD are right;
> the righteous walk in them.
>
> —HOSEA 14:9

> God will always give what is right to his people who cry to him night and day, and he will not be slow to answer them.
>
> —LUKE 18:7 NCV

When God locks a door, it needs to be locked. When he blocks a path, it needs to be blocked. When he stuck Paul and Silas in prison, God had a plan for the prison jailer. As Paul and Silas sang, God shook the prison. "At once all the prison doors flew open, and everyone's chains came loose" (Acts 16:26).

There God goes again, blasting open the most secure doors in town. When the jailer realized what had happened, he assumed all the prisoners had escaped. He drew his sword to take his life.

When Paul told him otherwise, the jailer brought the two missionaries out and asked, "What must I do to be saved?" (Acts 16:30). Paul told him to believe. He did, and he and all his family were baptized. The jailer washed their wounds, and Jesus washed his sins. God shut the door of the jail cell so that he could open the heart of the jailer.

God uses closed doors to advance his cause.

He closed the womb of a young Sarah so he could display his power to the elderly one.

He shut the palace door on Moses the prince so he could open shackles through Moses the liberator.

He marched Daniel out of Jerusalem so he could use Daniel in Babylon.

And Jesus. Yes, even Jesus knew the challenge of a blocked door. When he requested a path that bypassed the cross, God said no. He said no to Jesus in the garden of Gethsemane so he could say yes to us at the gates of heaven.

God's goal is people. He'll stir up a storm to display

his power. He'll keep you out of Asia so you'll speak to Lydia. He'll place you in prison so you'll talk to the jailer. He might even sideline a quarterback in the biggest game of the season. This happened in the 2010 BCS National Championship Game. Colt McCoy, the University of Texas quarterback, had enjoyed four years of open doors. He was the winningest signal caller in the history of collegiate football. But in the National Championship Game, the most important contest of his university career, a shoulder injury put him out of the game in the first quarter. "Slam" went the door. Colt spent most of the game in the locker room.

I don't know if he, like Paul and Silas, was singing, but we know he was trusting. For after the game, he said these words:

> I love this game.... I've done everything I can to contribute to my team.... It's unfortunate I didn't get to play. I would have given everything I had to be out there with my team. But ... I always give God the glory. I never question why things happen the way they do. God is in control of my life. And I know that, if nothing else, I'm standing on the rock.[25]

Even on a bad night, Colt gave testimony to a good

God. Did God close the door on the game so he could open the door of a heart?

Colt's father would say so. A young football player approached Brad McCoy after he returned from the game and asked, "I heard what your son said after the game, but I have one question. What is the rock?" McCoy responded, "Well, son, we sing about him at church," and began singing the hymn:

> My hope is built on nothing less
> Than Jesus' blood and righteousness.
> I dare not trust the sweetest frame,
> but wholly lean on Jesus' Name.
> On Christ, the solid Rock, I stand,
> All other ground is sinking sand;
> All other ground is sinking sand.[26]

It's not that our plans are bad but that God's plans are better.

"My thoughts are nothing like your thoughts,"
  says the LORD.
"And my ways are far beyond anything you
  could imagine.

> For just as the heavens are higher than the
>   earth,
>   so my ways are higher than your ways
>   and my thoughts higher than your thoughts."
>
> —ISAIAH 55:8–9 NLT

This is what I'm trying to teach Molly. Our family blocks doors so she can have better doors.

And this is what God is trying to teach us. Your blocked door doesn't mean God doesn't love you. Quite the opposite. It's proof that he does.

Kayla, 15—Oftentimes we as human beings don't like being told no by our parents, friends, or coworkers, and we try everything in our possible state of mind to change their answers. Most likely their answer will still be no. But when God says no to us, we sometimes sit and wonder, *Why?* We hear that God is all-powerful and merciful. The Bible says ask and it shall be given. In our heads that sometimes translates to "God will give me anything I want as long as I say please," but in life that isn't true. Yes, God has the power to give you anything you desire, but within reason. There are some things that we want in life but don't need, and God is there to help us decide between the two. Even when the door you want to walk through is blocked, the open door God will lead you to is closer than you think.

DON'T JUST SIT THERE ...

Thank God that he sometimes writes the story of your life differently than you would have by blocking some doors. Ask him to help you to trust him when it's a door you really wanted to go through.

Ask your parents about some of the things they wanted to do in their lives that they just could not make happen because it became impossible. How do they feel about those blocked doors now: regretful or grateful that they could not go that way?

Think about the last story you read or saw in a movie. Write down what the hero wanted to happen. Then write down what got in the way. On a scale of one to ten, write down a number representing how interesting the story would have been if everything had happened exactly as the hero wanted it without any conflict or struggle.

Ask a friend to tell you the story of their life. Listen for the blocked doors that help to determine which direction the story will take.

Ask a wise Christian you know to tell you how they go about making hard decisions in life. How do they try to figure out what is God's will for their story?

CHAPTER 9

WHEN GOD'S STORY
BECOMES YOURS ...

ALL THINGS
WORK
FOR GOOD

THINK ABOUT IT!

What genre is the story you're in right now? Is your life a romantic comedy or a horror story? Are you the hero of a great adventure or the damsel in distress? Maybe it's a sports film or a war movie or a documentary in which everything is always "real."

Here's a secret: You can almost always change the genre to whatever you want it to be just by changing your attitude toward your everyday circumstances.

Those convinced the world is out to get them will see every bad thing that happens as the next chapter in their own personal slasher film. People who believe there is no plan for the universe, no Storyteller, may simply see the events of their boring, everyday existence as so much documentary footage that needs to be edited into whatever context they decide matters to them.

But those of us who are convinced that God is writing our story, that he is up to something in the universe and has cast us in the role of helping to accomplish his purposes, will see our stories as the grandest of adventures even on the worst days. We will always be asking, "How will this moment lead to the good ending I know God is writing?"

Lloyd—I was a week from going on a vacation to Sea World, [and] I was anxious to get to San Antonio. I was over at my grandparents when my grandfather got a call from my cousin that my great-aunt had died leaving the hospital. The vacation was called off. I was heartbroken that we were going to a funeral instead of vacation. I lost sight of the truth; blinded by anger and sadness, I felt lost like there was no one there.

ROBBEN ISLAND CONSISTS OF THREE SQUARE MILES OF windswept land off the southern tip of Africa. Over the centuries it has served as the home for a prison, leper colony, mental asylum, and naval base. Most significantly, it was the home of one of the most famous political prisoners in history, Nelson Mandela.

He opposed the South African apartheid, a system designed to extend the rule and privileges of the white minority and diminish those of the blacks. It ensured that the 14 percent minority would control the rest of the population. Under apartheid, blacks were excluded from the "whites only" buses, "whites only" beaches, and "whites only" hospitals. Blacks could not run for office or live in a white neighborhood.

Apartheid legalized racism.

Mandela was the perfect man to challenge it. As a descendant of royalty, he was educated in the finest schools. As the son of a Christian mother, he embraced her love for God and people. Under the tutelage of a tribal chief, he learned the art of compromise and consensus. And as a young black lawyer in Cape Town, he experienced "a thousand slights, a thousand indignities, a thousand unremembered moments,"[27] which produced an inward fire to fight the system that imprisoned his people.

By the mid-1950s, Mandela was a force to be reckoned with. Passionate. Bitter. Given to retaliation. With his enviable pedigree and impressive stature (six feet two inches, 245 pounds), he was, for many, the hope of the black culture. But then came the events of August 5, 1962. Government officials arrested Mandela, convicted him of treason, and sent him to prison. For the next twenty-seven years, he stared through wired windows. And he wondered, surely he wondered, how a season in prison could play a part in God's plan.

You've asked such questions yourself. Not about your time in prison but about your time in a dead-end job, struggling church, puny town, or enfeebled body. Certain elements of life make sense. But what about autism, Alzheimer's, or Mandela's prison sentence on Robben Island? Was Paul including these conditions when he wrote Romans 8:28?

And we know that in all things God works for the good of those who love him, who have been called according to his purpose.

We know . . . There are so many things we do not know. We do not know if the economy will dip or if our team will win. We do not know what our parents are thinking or what career we will pursue. We don't even know "what we ought to pray for" (Romans 8:26). But according to Paul, we can be absolutely certain about four things. We know . . .

1. *God works.* He is busy behind the scenes, above the fray, within the fury. He hasn't checked out

or moved on. He is ceaseless and tireless. He never stops working.

2. *God works for the good.* Not for our comfort or pleasure or entertainment, but for our ultimate good. Since he is the ultimate good, would we expect anything less?

3. *God works for the good of those who love him.* Behold the benefit of loving God! Make his story your story, and your story takes on a happy ending. Guaranteed. Being the author of our salvation, he writes a salvation theme into our biography.

4. *God works in all things.* *Panta,* in Greek. Like "*panoramic*" or "*panacea*" or "*pandemic.*" All-inclusive. God works, not through a few things or through the good things, best things, or easy things. But in "all things" God works.

Puppet in the hands of fortune or fate? Not you. You are in the hands of a living, loving God. Random collection of disconnected short stories? Far from it. Your life is a crafted narrative written by a good God, who is working toward your supreme good.

God is not slipshod or haphazard. He planned creation

according to a calendar. He determined the details of salvation "before the foundation of the world" (1 Peter 1:20 NKJV). The death of Jesus was not an afterthought, nor was it Plan B or an emergency operation. Jesus died "when the set time had fully come" (Galatians 4:4), according to God's "deliberate plan and foreknowledge" (Acts 2:23).

God, in other words, isn't making up a plan as he goes along. Nor did he wind up the clock and walk away. "The Most High God rules the kingdom of mankind and sets over it whom he will" (Daniel 5:21 ESV). He "executes judgment, putting down one and lifting up another" (Psalm 75:7 ESV). "The LORD will not turn back until he has executed and accomplished the intentions of his mind" (Jeremiah 30:24 ESV). Look at those verbs: God *rules, sets, executes, accomplished.* These terms confirm the existence of heavenly blueprints and plans. Those plans include you. "In him we were also chosen, ... according to the plan of him who works out everything in conformity with the purpose of his will" (Ephesians 1:11).

This discovery changes everything! It changed the outlook of the mom Denalyn and I visited in the maternity ward two days ago. She had miscarried a child. Her face awash with tears and heart heavy with questions, she reached through the fog and held on to God's hand. "This will work out for good, won't it, Max?" I assured her it would, and reminded her of God's promise: "'For I know the plans I have for you,' declares the LORD, 'plans to prosper you and not to harm you, plans to give you hope and a future'" (Jeremiah 29:11).

The apostle Paul's life is proof. We know just enough of his story to see God's hand in each phase of it. Here is how Paul began his testimony: "I am indeed a Jew, born in Tarsus of Cilicia, but brought up in this city at the feet of Gamaliel, taught according to the strictness of our fathers' law, and was zealous toward God as you all are today" (Acts 22:3 NKJV).

Paul grew up in Tarsus. He called it "an important city" (Acts 21:39 NLT). He wasn't exaggerating. Tarsus sat only a few miles from the coast and served as a hub for sailors, pirates, and merchants from all sections of Europe and Asia. Any child raised in Tarsus would have heard a dozen languages and witnessed a tapestry of cultures.

Tarsus was also a depot city on the Roman highway system. The empire boasted a network of roads that connected business centers of the ancient world. Ephesus. Iconium. Derbe. Tarsus. Syrian Antioch and Caesarea. While young Paul likely didn't visit these cities, he grew up hearing about them. Tarsus instilled a Mediterranean map in his heart and a keen intellect in his mind. Tarsus rivaled the academic seats of Alexandria and Athens.

Paul conversed with students in the streets, and, at the right age, became one himself. He learned the common language of his day: Greek. He mastered it. He spoke it. He wrote it. He thought it.

Paul not only spoke the international language of the world; he carried its passport. He was born a Jew and a Roman citizen. Whenever he traveled through the empire, he was entitled to all the rights and privileges of a Roman citizen. He could enter any port and demand a judicial hearing. He could even appeal to Caesar. He was treated, not as a slave or foreigner, but as a freeman. How did his father acquire such a status? Perhaps in exchange for tents. Paul, himself a tentmaker, likely learned his craft from his father, who probably created durable gear for the ever-mobile Roman soldiers.

Young Paul left Tarsus with everything an itinerant missionary would need: cultural familiarity, linguistic skills, documents for travel, and a trade for earning a living. That was only the beginning.

Paul's parents sent him to Jerusalem for rabbinical studies. He memorized large sections of the Torah and digested massive amounts of rabbinical law. He was a valedictorian-level student, a Hebrew of Hebrews. Paul later wrote: "I was advancing in Judaism beyond many of my own age among my people, so extremely zealous was I for the traditions of my fathers" (Galatians 1:14 ESV).

An interesting side note. Paul and Jesus may have passed each other on the streets of Jerusalem. If Paul was a member of the Sanhedrin court when he persecuted the church, he would have been at least thirty years old, the minimum-age requirement for being a member of the court. That would make him roughly the same age as Jesus, who was crucified in his early thirties. Which raises this fanciful question: Did young Paul and young Jesus find themselves in Jerusalem at the same time? A twelve-year-old Messiah and his father. A young Saul and his studies. If so, did the Christ at some point cast a glance at his future apostle-to-be?

We know God did. Before Paul was following God, God was leading Paul. He gave him an education, a vocation, the necessary documentation. He schooled Paul in the law of Moses and the language of Greece. Who better to present Jesus as the fulfillment of the law than a scholar of the law?

But what about Paul's violence? He confessed: "I persecuted this Way to the death, binding and delivering into prisons both men and women" (Acts 22:4 NKJV). He tore husbands from their homes and moms from their children. He declared jihad against the church and spilled the blood of disciples. Could God use this ugly chapter to advance his cause?

More than a hypothetical question. We all have seasons that are hard to explain. Before we knew God's story, we made a mess of our own. Even afterward, we're prone to demand our own way, cut our own path, and hurt people in the process. Can God make good out of our bad?

He did with Paul.

> "Now it happened, as I journeyed and came near Damascus at about noon, suddenly a great light from heaven shone around me. And I fell to the ground and heard a voice saying to me ..."
>
> —ACTS 22:6–7 NKJV

"I'm going to give you a taste of your own medicine."
"Back to the dust with you, you Christian-killer."
"Prepare to meet your Maker!"

Did Paul expect to hear words like these? Regardless, he didn't. Even before he requested mercy, he was offered mercy. Jesus told him:

> "I have a job for you. I've handpicked you to be

a servant and witness to what's happened today, and
to what I'm going to show you.

I'm sending you off to open the eyes of the outsid-
ers so they can see.... I'm sending you off to present
my offer of sins forgiven, and a place in the family."

—ACTS 26:16–18 MSG

Jesus transformed Paul, the card-carrying legalist, into
a champion for mercy. Who would have thought? Yet who
would be better qualified? Paul could write epistles of grace
by dipping his pen into the inkwell of his own heart. He'd
learned Greek in the schools of Tarsus, tentmaking in the
home of his father, the Torah at the feet of Gamaliel. And
he learned about love when Jesus paid him a personal visit
on Damascus Highway.

"All things" worked together.

Bethany, 15—I was in an accident this year that really
did change my life. I hit my head and lost memory of literally
everybody I knew. I was mad at God for a really, really long
time. Slowly, over time, my memory came back. That whole
experience made me realize how much I put everything in my
memory before him. So he literally swiped it all away and set my
priorities straight. Now my life revolves around mission work.
Best thing that ever happened to me.

I saw an example of this process in our kitchen. My intent was to chat with Denalyn about some questions. She was stirring up a delicacy for someone's birthday. She assured me she could talk and bake at the same time. So I talked. She baked. But as she baked, I stopped talking.

Had I never witnessed the creation of cuisine? *Au contraire!* I've applauded the society of Julia Child since I was a child. We who do not cook stand in awe of those who do. And I did.

Denalyn buzzed about the kitchen like the queen of the hive. She snatched boxes off the shelves, pulled bowls out of the pantry. I've been known to stare at an open refrigerator for days in search of mayonnaise or ketchup. Not Denalyn. She grabbed the carton of eggs with one hand and butter with the other, never pausing to look.

She positioned the ingredients and utensils on the table as a surgeon would her tools. Once everything was in place, off she went. Eggs cracking, yolks dropping. Shake this, stir that. Pour out the milk. Measure the sugar. Sift, mix, and beat. She was a blur of hands and elbows, a conductor of the kitchen, the Cleopatra of cuisine, the da Vinci of da kitchen, the lord of the lard, the boss of the bakery.

She popped the pan into the oven, turned the knob to 350 degrees, wiped her hands with a towel, turned to me, and said the words I longed to hear: "Want to lick the bowl?" I fell at her feet and called her blessed. Well, maybe not. But I did lick the bowl, spatula, and beaters. And I did wonder if Denalyn's work in the kitchen is a picture of God's work in us.

All the transfers, layoffs, breakdowns, breakups, and breakouts. Difficulties. Opportunities. Sifted and stirred and popped into the oven. Heaven knows, we've felt the heat. We've wondered if God's choice of ingredients will result in anything worth serving.

If Nelson Mandela did, no one could blame him. His prison life was harsh. He was confined to a six-by-six-foot concrete room. It had one small window that overlooked the courtyard. He had a desk, a mattress, a chair, three blankets, and a rusted-iron sanitary bucket for washing and shaving. Meals came from corn: breakfast was a porridge of corn scraped from the cob; lunch and supper consisted of corn on the cob; coffee was roasted corn mixed with water.

Mandela and the other prisoners were awakened at 5:30 a.m. They crushed rocks into gravel until noon, ate lunch, then worked until 4:00 p.m. Back in the cell at 5:00, asleep by 8:00. Discrimination continued even in the prison. Africans, like Mandela, were required to wear short pants and were denied bread.

Yet God used it all to shape Mandela. The prisoner read widely: Leo Tolstoy, John Steinbeck, Daphne du Maurier. He exercised daily: a hundred fingertip push-ups, two hundred sit-ups, fifty deep knee bends. Most of all he honed the capacity to compromise and forgive. He developed courtesy in all situations, disarming even the guards who had been placed to trouble him. He became particularly close to one jailer who, over two decades, read the Bible and discussed Scripture with Mandela. "'All men,' Mandela reflected later, 'have a core of decency, and ... if their heart is touched, they are capable of changing.'"[28]

After twenty-seven years of confinement, at the age of seventy-two, Mandela was released. Those who knew him well described the pre-prison Mandela as "cocky and pugnacious." But the refined Mandela? "I came out mature," he said. He was devoted to "rationality, logic, and compromise." Journalists noted his lack of bitterness. Others observed that he was "unmarred by rancor."[29] Within four years Mandela was elected president and set out to lead South Africa out of apartheid and into a new era of equality.

God needed an educated, sophisticated leader who'd mastered the art of patience and compromise, so he tempered Mandela in prison.

He needed a culture-crossing, Greek-speaking, border-passing, Torah-quoting, self-supporting missionary, so he gave grace to Paul, and Paul shared grace with the world.

And you? In a moment before moments, your Maker looked into the future and foresaw the needs and demands of your generation. He instilled, and is instilling, within you everything you need to fulfill his plan in this era. "God made us to do good works, which God planned in advance for us to live our lives doing" (Ephesians 2:10 NCV).

If that doesn't take the cake, I don't know what does.

Morgan—God has played a pretty big role in my life. So far. I have gone to church ever since I can remember. I feel like through the trials of my life I have gotten closer to him—though my trials aren't very big on the spectrum of "bad things" that could have happened. But for me, these were the hard times in my life. In some way we will eventually be able to use all of our experiences to further his kingdom or to reach out to people; yes, the bad things happen, but they are there for good. God has an amazing way of using the worst situations and things that have happened for good and growing in the end.

DON'T JUST SIT THERE . . .

Write out Romans 8:28 on a piece of paper. Ask yourself and answer honestly, "Do I believe God works in my life? Do I believe he works for my good? Do I love him? Am I called for his purposes?" If you said no to any of those questions, talk to a wise Christian you trust to try to figure out why.

Thank God that he is now and always has been at work in your story, for your good, in everything that has happened and will happen to you.

If you have never read *The Horse and His Boy* by C. S. Lewis (or if it has been a long time), consider reading it soon. Notice how Aslan is at work in the lives of the heroes even when they are not aware of it.

Text Romans 8:28 to two or three Christian friends and ask if they think it's true for their life. When they respond, text back, "Why?"

If you know someone who has been through something terrible that you would never want to experience and yet still seems to trust God and enjoy him, ask that person about this verse. Why does she believe it?

Make a quick list of two or three of the worst things that have happened in your story so far. Circle the ones you are sure that God helped you through and that he was using for your good.

CHAPTER 10

WHEN GOD'S STORY
BECOMES YOURS ...

GOD WILL
COME FOR YOU

THINK ABOUT IT!

You likely can think of a few stories you loved while you were reading or watching them that quickly fell off your list of favorites when you got to the ending. A lousy ending is the most painful way to ruin an otherwise awesome story.

Here's a promise from the Storyteller: Your story won't end that way. In fact, it will be just the opposite. No matter how you feel about the way your story in God's bigger story is going right now, you will not in any way be disappointed with the final chapter.

Every loose end will be tied up. Every heroic act will be rewarded. Every villain will be appropriately punished. And the Father will welcome home his brave protagonists, drying their tears and promising to live with them forevermore.

Have you read ahead to the ending? You should. It won't ruin the story. It will only make it more fun. That's another promise.

With hopes of earning extra cash, my dad once took a three-month job assignment in New England. I was ten years old, midway between training wheels and girlfriends. I thought much about baseball and bubble gum. Can't say I ever thought once about Bangor, Maine. Until Dad went there.

When he did, I found the town on the map. I calculated the distance between the Texas plains and the lobster coast. My teacher let me write a report on Henry Wadsworth Longfellow, and Dad sent us a jug of maple syrup. Our family lived in two worlds, ours and his.

We talked much about my father's pending return. "When Dad comes back, we will ... fix the basketball net ... take a trip to Grandma's ... stay up later." Mom used his coming to comfort and caution. She could do both with the same phrase. With soft assurance, "Your dad will be home soon." Or clenched teeth, "Your dad will be home soon." She circled his arrival date on the calendar and crossed out each day as it passed. She made it clear: Dad's coming would be a big deal.

It was. Four decades have weathered the memories, but these remain: the sudden smell of Old Spice in the house; his deep, bellowing voice; gifts all around; and a happy sense of settledness. Dad's return changed everything.

The return of Christ will do likewise.

Jude has a name for this event: "the great Day" (Jude 6).

The great Day will be a normal day. People will drink coffee, endure traffic snarls, laugh at jokes, and take note of the weather. Thousands of people will be born; thousands will die.

The Arrival of the Son of Man will take place in times like Noah's. Before the great flood everyone was carrying on as usual, having a good time right up to the day Noah boarded the ark. They knew nothing—until the flood hit and swept everything away.

—MATTHEW 24:37–39 MSG

The tourists of Thailand's coast come to mind. They spent the morning of December 26, 2004, applying suntan lotion and throwing beach balls, unaware that a tsunami-stirred wave was moving toward them at the speed of a jetliner. Christ's coming will be equally unexpected. Most people will be oblivious, playing on the beach.

His shout will get our attention. "For the Lord Himself will descend from heaven with a shout" (1 Thessalonians 4:16 NKJV). Before we see angels, hear trumpets, or embrace our grandparents, we will be engulfed by Jesus' voice. John heard the voice of God and compared it to "the sound of many waters" (Revelation 1:15 NKJV). Perhaps you've stood at the base of a cataract so loud and full of fury that you had to shout to be heard. Or maybe you've heard the roar of a lion. When the king of beasts opens his mouth, every head in the jungle lifts. The King of kings will prompt the same response: "The Lord will roar from on high" (Jeremiah 25:30).

Lazarus heard such a roar. His body was entombed and his soul in paradise when Jesus shouted into both places: "[Jesus] cried with a loud voice, 'Lazarus, come forth!' And he who had died came out" (John 11:43–44 NKJV). Expect the same shout and shaking of the corpses on the great Day. "The dead will hear the voice of the

Son of God.... All who are ... in their graves will hear his voice. Then they will come out" (John 5:25, 28–29 NCV).

The shout of God will trigger the "voice of an archangel ... with the trumpet of God" (1 Thessalonians 4:16 NKJV). The archangel is the commanding officer. He will dispatch armies of angels to their greatest mission: to gather the children of God into one great assemblage. Envision these silvered messengers spilling out of the heavens into the atmosphere. You'll more quickly count the winter snowflakes than you will number these hosts. Jude announced that "the Lord is coming with thousands and thousands of holy angels to judge everyone" (verses 14–15 CEV). The population of God's armies was too high for John to count. He saw "ten thousand times ten thousand, and thousands of thousands" (Revelation 5:11 NKJV).

They minister to the saved and battle the devil. They keep you safe and clear your path. "He has put his angels in charge of you to watch over you wherever you go" (Psalm 91:11 NCV). And on the great Day, they will escort you into the skies, where you will meet God. "He'll dispatch the angels; they will pull in the chosen from the four winds, from pole to pole" (Mark 13:27 MSG).

Whether you are in Peoria or paradise, if you're a follower of Jesus, you can count on an angelic chaperone into the greatest gathering in history. We assume the demons will gather the rebellious. We aren't told. We are told, however, that the saved and lost alike will witness the assembly. "All the nations will be gathered before him" (Matthew 25:32).

The Population Reference Bureau estimates that 106 billion people have been born since the dawn of the human race.[30] Every single one of them will stand in the great assembly of souls. He who made us will convene us. "The LORD, who scattered his people, will gather them" (Jeremiah 31:10 NLT). "All the ends of the earth shall see the salvation of our God" (Isaiah 52:10 ESV).

At some point in this grand collection, our spirits will be reunited with our bodies:

> It will happen in a moment, in the blink of an eye, when the last trumpet is blown. For when the trumpet sounds, those who have died will be raised to live forever. And we who are living will also be transformed. For our dying bodies must be transformed into bodies that will never die; our mortal bodies must be transformed into immortal bodies.
>
> —1 CORINTHIANS 15:52–53 NLT

Paradise will give up her souls.

The earth will give up her dead, and the sky will stage a reunion of spirit and flesh. As our souls reenter our bodies, a massive sound will erupt around us: "On that day heaven will pass away with a roaring sound. Everything that makes up the universe will burn and be destroyed. The earth and everything that people have done on it will be exposed" (2 Peter 3:10 GWT).

Jesus called this "the re-creation of the world" (Matthew 19:28 MSG). God will purge every square inch that sin has contaminated, polluted, degraded, or defiled. But we may not even notice the reconstruction, for an even greater sight will appear before us: "the Son of Man coming on the clouds in the sky with power and great glory" (Matthew 24:30 GWT).

God has often used clouds to indicate his presence. He led the Israelites with a cloudy pillar. He spoke to Moses through the mist on Sinai, and to Jesus through the cloud at the transfiguration. Clouds symbolize his hiddenness, but on the great Day they will declare his visible presence. Note the preposition: "the Son of Man coming *on* the clouds" (emphasis mine). Subtle distinction. Great declaration. Every person, prince, pauper, saint, sinner — every eye will see Jesus. "All the nations will be gathered before him" (Matthew 25:32).

Sydney —It can be daunting to think about God's return. I kind of think of the apocalyptic movies when I think of his return. I start feeling anxious and scared, especially thinking that my world and some people I love will be gone. But what gives me relief is the idea found in the analogy of Max not knowing what his father was doing in Maine. God is doing something great, something I can't wrap my mind around. And whatever that is, it will be for the eternal happiness of those he loves.

By this point we will have seen much: the flurry of angels, the ascension of the bodies, the great gathering of the nations. We will have heard much: the shout of God and the angel, the trumpet blast, and the purging explosion. But every sight and sound will seem a remote memory compared to what will happen next: "He will be King and sit on his great throne" (Matthew 25:31 NCV).

This is the direction in which all of history is focused. This is the moment toward which God's plot is moving. The details, characters, antagonists, heroes, and subplots all arc in this direction. God's story carries us toward a coronation for which all of creation groans:

For everything, absolutely everything, above and below, visible and invisible, rank after rank after rank of angels—*everything* got started in him and finds its purpose in him.... He was supreme in the beginning and—leading the resurrection parade—he is supreme in the end.

—COLOSSIANS 1:16, 18 MSG

God's creation will return to its beginning: a one-king kingdom. Our earth is plagued by multiple competing monarchs, each one of us climbing ladders and claiming thrones. But we will gladly remove our crowns when Christ comes back for us.

During one of the crusades, Philippe Auguste, king of France, gathered his noble knights and men to call them to be strong in battle. He placed his crown on a table with the inscription "To the most worthy." He pledged the crown as the prize to be given the bravest fighter.

They went to battle and returned victorious and encircled the table on which the crown had been placed. One of the nobles stepped forward, took the crown, and put it on the head of the king, saying, "Thou, O King, art the most worthy."[31]

On the great Day you'll hear billions of voices make the identical claim about Jesus Christ. "Every knee will bow to the name of Jesus—everyone in heaven, on earth, and under the earth. And everyone will confess that Jesus Christ is Lord" (Philippians 2:10–11 NCV).

Multitudes of people will bow low like a field of wind-blown wheat, each one saying, "Thou, O King, art the most worthy."

There will be one monumental difference. Some people will continue the confession they began on earth. They will crown Christ again, gladly. Others will crown him for the first time. They will do so sadly. They denied Christ on earth, so he will deny them in heaven.

But those who accepted him will live with God forever. "I heard a voice thunder from the Throne: 'Look! Look! God has moved into the neighborhood, making his home with men and women! They're his people, he's their God'" (Revelation 21:3 MSG). The narrator makes the same point four times in four consecutive phrases:

> "God has moved into the neighborhood"
>
> "making his home with men and women"
>
> "They're his people"
>
> "he's their God"

The announcement comes with the energy of a six-year-old declaring the arrival of his father from a long trip. "Daddy's home! He's here! Mom, he's back!" One statement won't suffice. This is big news worthy of repetition.

We shall finally see God face-to-face. "They will see his face" (Revelation 22:4).

Let this sink in. You will see the face of God. You will look into the eyes of the One who has always seen; you will behold the mouth that commands history. And if there is anything more amazing than the moment you see his face, it's the moment he touches yours. "He will wipe every tear from their eyes" (Revelation 21:4).

God will touch your tears. Not flex his muscles or show off his power. Lesser kings would strut their stallions or give a victory speech. Not God. He prefers to rub a thumb across your cheek as if to say, "There, there ... no more tears."

Isn't that what a father does?

There was much I didn't understand about my father's time in Maine. The responsibilities of his job, his daily activities, the reason he needed to go. I was too young to comprehend all the details. But I knew this much: he would come home.

By the same token, who can understand what God is doing? These days on earth can seem so difficult: marred by conflict, saddened by separation. We fight, pollute, discriminate, and kill. *What is this world coming to?* we wonder. God's answer: a great Day. On the great Day all of history will be consummated in Christ. He will assume his position "far above all rule and authority and power and dominion ... not only in this age but also in the one to come" (Ephesians 1:21 NASB). And he, the Author of it all, will close the book on this life and open the book to the next and begin to read to us from his unending story.

Robert, 18—Sometimes a good story can be a good story without a good ending. Not everyone wants every superhero to win every time. I would like to see the bad guy win at least once and rule until the next movie or book when the villain is finally overthrown. I guess that's a lot like God's story. Satan loves his small triumphs, but they won't last forever.

The idea of Jesus returning doesn't scare me, because I believe that he will take me with him. Jesus returning would be the best thing that could ever happen to anyone, because I know that every human/soul wants to be in heaven with our Father. Yes, this does excite me, because I love him so much that I want him to come back and take me with him.

DON'T JUST SIT THERE ...

Thank God for including you in his story, especially the part described in this chapter.

Think of three friends who don't know God's story or who have not trusted in Jesus. Circle one whom you are willing to pray for and talk to about how Jesus has changed your story.

Write out Revelation 21:1–5 and ask one of your parents if you can read it to them. Ask what these verses make them think about.

Got any money? Find a missionary or organization whose goal is to tell people how to be with the Father in eternity forever, and give them some of your funds so you can help.

Make a list of all the things you did yesterday and circle the ones that will still matter on the day God will wipe away every tear and make his home with us. Draw an X through the ones you decide aren't worth doing tomorrow.

Ask God to give you the courage to live for him in the part of his story he has included you in today.

WHEN GOD'S STORY BECOMES YOURS ...

YOU WILL FINALLY GRADUATE

MAY 19, 2007, WAS A SPLENDID NIGHT FOR AN OUTDOOR graduation. The South Texas sky was as blue as a robin's egg. A just-passed rain shower perfumed the air. Thirty-four members of the Lucado clan occupied a sizable section of the amphitheater seats in honor of high-school-graduating Sara, my youngest daughter.

Never accused of timidity, we Lucados attempted to do the wave as Sara walked across the platform. We more closely resembled popping popcorn ... but Sara heard our support. Graduation warrants such displays. There's nothing small about the transfer of tassels. Cut the cake and call the newspaper. Applaud the closing, not of a chapter, but of a tome. Graduation is no small matter.

What we didn't know, however, is that two Lucado

women were graduating the same evening. About the same time Sara stepped across the platform, my mom stepped into paradise. Sara and Thelma, separated in age by seventy-six years, yet joined by the same graduation date.

Applause for the first. Tears for the second. *Hooray* for Sara. *Oh my* about Mom. Gladness. Sadness. The sorrow is understandable. Reactions to graduation and death shouldn't be identical.

Yet should they be so different?

Both celebrate completion and transition. And both gift the graduate with recognition: a diploma to one and a brand-new life to the other.

It will take only a second—as quickly as an eye blinks—when the last trumpet sounds. The trumpet will sound and those who have died will be raised to live forever, and we will all be changed. This body that can be destroyed must clothe itself with something that can never be destroyed. And this body that dies must clothe itself with something that can never die.

—1 CORINTHIANS 15:52–53 NCV

As God's story becomes your story, you make this

wonderful discovery: you will graduate from this life into heaven. Jesus' plan is to "gather together in one all things in Christ" (Ephesians 1:10 NKJV). "All things" includes your body. Your eyes that read this book. Your hands that hold it. Your blood-pumping heart, arm-hinging elbow, weight-supporting torso. God will reunite your body with your soul and create something unlike anything you have seen: an eternal body.

You will finally be healthy. You never have been. Even on the days you felt fine, you weren't. You were a sitting duck for disease, infections, airborne bacteria, and microbes. And what of you on your worst days?

Last Sunday as I sat in front of our church, my eyes seemed to radar toward the physically challenged. A recent retiree with a rush of white hair just found out about a brain tumor. So did a thirtyish mother of three. "I thought it was a migraine," she had told me earlier in the week.

Philip is in law school and a wheelchair. I haven't seen Adam in several weeks. He's a Juilliard grad. Multiple sclerosis has silenced his keyboard. Doctors are giving another member two months to live.

I hate disease. I'm sick of it.

So is Christ. Consider his response to the suffering of a deaf mute. "He took him aside from the multitude, and put His fingers in his ears, and He spat and touched his tongue. Then, looking up to heaven, He sighed, and said to him, 'Ephphatha,' that is, 'Be opened' " (Mark 7:33 – 34 NKJV).

Everything about this healing stands out. The way Jesus separates the man from the crowd. The tongue and ear touching. The presence of Aramaic in the Greek account. But it's the sigh that we notice. Jesus looked up to heaven and sighed. This is a sigh of sadness, a deep breath, and a heavenly glance that resolves, "It won't be this way for long."

Jesus will heal all who seek healing in him. There are no exceptions to this promise — no nuances, fine-print conditions, or caveats. To say some will be healed beyond the grave by no means diminishes the promise. The truth is this: "When Christ appears, *we shall be like him*, for we shall see him as he is" (1 John 3:2, emphasis mine).

"We shall be like him." Let every parent of a Down syndrome or wheelchair-bound child write these words on the bedroom wall. Let the disabled, infected, bedridden, and anemic put themselves to sleep with the promise "We shall be like him." Let amputees and the atrophied take this promise to heart: "We shall be like him." We shall graduate from this version of life into his likeness.

You'll have a spiritual body. In your current state,

your flesh battles your spirit. Your eyes look where they shouldn't. Your taste buds desire the wrong drinks. Your heart knows you shouldn't be anxious, but your mind still worries. Can't we relate to Paul's confession? "I truly delight in God's commands, but it's pretty obvious that not all of me joins in that delight. Parts of me covertly rebel, and just when I least expect it, they take charge" (Romans 7:22–23 MSG).

Your "parts" will no longer rebel in heaven. Your new body will be a spiritual body, with all members cooperating toward one end. Joni Eareckson Tada's words are powerful on this point. She has been confined to a wheelchair since the age of seventeen. Yet the greatest heavenly attraction for her is not new legs but a new soul.

I can't wait to be clothed in righteousness. Without a trace of sin. True, it will be wonderful to stand, stretch, and reach to the sky, but it will be more wonderful to offer praise that is pure. I won't be crippled by distractions. Disabled by insincerity. I won't be handicapped by a ho-hum halfheartedness. My heart will join with yours and bubble over with effervescent adoration. We will finally be able to fellowship fully with the Father and the Son.

For me, this will be the best part of heaven.[32]

In heaven "there shall be no more curse" (Revelation 22:3 NKJV). As much as we hate carcinomas and cardiac arrests, don't we hate sin even more? Cystic fibrosis steals breath, but selfishness and stinginess steal joy. Diabetes can ruin the system of a body, but deceit, denial, and distrust are ruining society.

Heaven, however, has scheduled a graduation. Sin will no longer be at war with our flesh. Eyes won't lust, thoughts won't wander, hands won't steal, our minds won't judge, appetites won't rage, and our tongues won't lie. We will be brand new.

Some of you live in such road-weary bodies: knees ache, eyes dim, skin sags. Others exited the womb on an uphill ride. While I have no easy answers for your struggle, I implore you to see your challenge in the scope of God's story. View these days on earth as but the opening lines of his sweeping saga. Let's stand with Paul on the promise of eternity.

> So we're not giving up. How could we! Even though on the outside it often looks like things are falling apart on us, on the inside, where God is making new life, not a day goes by without his unfolding grace. These hard times are small potatoes compared to the

coming good times, the lavish celebration prepared for us. There's far more here than meets the eye. The things we see now are here today, gone tomorrow. But the things we can't see now will last forever.

—2 CORINTHIANS 4:16–18 MSG

I write these words during the final hours of a two-week vacation. I've passed the last dozen days with my favorite people, my wife and daughters. We've watched the sun set, fish jump, and waves crash. We've laughed at old stories and made new memories. A trip for the ages.

At its inception, however, I got searched at airport security. I removed my shoes and handed my boarding pass to the official. He instructed me to step over to the side. I groaned as he waved his wand over my body. Why single me out? Isn't it enough that we have to plod barefoot through a scanner? Do they think I am a terrorist? You can tell that I don't like the moments at airport security. But as I remember this vacation, I won't reflect on its irritating inauguration. It was necessary but quickly lost in the splendor of the vacation.

You suppose we'll someday say the same words about this life? "Necessary but quickly lost in the splendor of heaven." I have a hunch we will. We'll see death differently

too. We'll remember the day we died with the same fond-
ness we remember graduation day.

By the way, if I graduate before you do, you'll see me
waiting for you. I'll be the one in the stands starting the
wave.

WHERE GOD'S STORY AND YOUR STORY COLLIDE

CHAPTER 1

ORDINARY MATTERS

1. What are some ways you have seen God use ordinary people to accomplish his purposes?

2. Do you feel that most teenagers would take offense at being called "ordinary"? Why or why not?

3. What do you think is the difference between being ordinary and recognizing how amazingly God has created each of us as individuals?

4. What are some of the ways in which Jesus, as the Son of God, is not at all ordinary? What makes him God? (If you need help, check out Colossians 1:15 – 20.)

5. Max imagines what the innkeeper *might* have said when confronted with the truth about Mary. How do you think you would have reacted to the news that God was inside a teenage girl? Have you ever reacted like that innkeeper to things that happen today? How did you deal with those moments?

6. If Jesus came today, how would people perceive him? How do you think today's reality TV and celebrity culture would affect Jesus' mission on earth?

7. Did we deserve for God to become one of us, an ordinary human being, in order to save us? Why or why not?

8. Would you feel the same about Jesus if he had not become an ordinary person like us (while staying fully God)? Why does his becoming human matter to us so much?

9. It's a big deal to us that Jesus became one of us. It helps us to know that he understands what it's like to be human. Why do you think it was important to God to send Jesus as a man?

10. Who are some of the ordinary people in your life whom God has used to help you in some huge ways? Does someone have to be special to be used by God for things that really matter?

CHAPTER 2

YOU KNOW
SATAN'S NEXT MOVE

1. Do you feel that most people your age believe that Satan is real? Why or why not?

2. Does acknowledging Satan's existence change the way you live each day? Do you think it should? (Check out 1 Peter 5:8 for help with this one.)

3. What is the danger of living like the devil isn't interested in your life?

4. Do you think most of your friends believe in the devil? How do you think their positions on this issue impact their lives?

5. If you know a lot about how the devil is described in the Bible, can you see ways that some of the best fictional villains are like him? Do they resent the hero getting all of the glory? Is deception one of their best weapons?

6. What was Satan's strategy when he brought three temptations to Jesus in the desert?

7. The Bible calls the devil and those beings on his side our "enemy." Do you think they know your weaknesses? How might they use your weaknesses against you?

8. How did Jesus counter the temptation attacks that Satan brought against him? How could you use Jesus' strategy to do the same thing?

9. One of the devil's strategies is to get us to question the truth. Have you ever encountered doubts in your life? How do you respond to them?

10. Do you think the devil gets blamed for things he doesn't do? Why?

CHAPTER 3

YOU FIND YOUR
TRUE HOME

1. What makes home "home" for you?

2. What are some of the things that people think will finally make them happy and at home in this life if they can just get to them?

3. Is it wrong to want the best things in this life in order to make ourselves more comfortable, more at home?

4. So what is the problem with living for — or putting our hope in — money or success or friendship or sex or family or sports or fun to make us truly happy?

5. Where do true happiness and satisfaction come from? Why does it make sense to expect that we'll find ultimate happiness and satisfaction in eternity with God?

6. In what ways do you long for the home God offers us in eternity? What will be there that we do not have here?

7. What questions do you have about your eternal home in heaven?

8. In what ways do you see others disappointed because their present world is dissatisfying?

9. If you already believe your true home is in heaven, why do you think we still struggle so much with believing we'd finally be fully happy here "if only" we could get some other thing?

10. What are some things God does for us here in this life to help us to have joy and peace and purpose until we get to eternity with him?

CHAPTER 4

YOU HEAR A VOICE
YOU CAN TRUST

1. In many fictional stories the main character encounters a mentor, teacher, or wise person to help figure out the best way to live. What do mentors help their students achieve? What mentors do you have in your life?

2. The disciples left their lives to follow Jesus, and they really had no idea who he was yet. Why do you think they followed him? What would make you decide to follow someone you hardly knew?

3. Whose voices do you know you can trust to steer you in the right direction?

4. Why have you come to trust those people?

5. What are some voices in your life that have let you down or led you in a wrong direction?

6. Is there any one person in your life who is completely right all of the time? Could a trusted person lead you astray if they were wrong and didn't realize it?

7. How is trusting Jesus as God (and trusting the Bible as truth) different from trusting the wise people in your life?

8. Are you convinced that the direction God steers you will never be wrong?

9. What's the difference between really trusting someone and just agreeing with them about the best direction? (Hint: Think about the story of the blind pilot.)

10. Do you think we sometimes believe we're trusting God's direction when we really just happen to be going that way because it also makes sense to us? Has your faith in him ever been tested because his way didn't make any sense to you?

CHAPTER 5

YOU WON'T BE
FORSAKEN

1. Here's a hard question: How much guilt do you carry around with you? Is there one bad thing (or several bad things) you've done — or that you still want to do — that is always on your mind?

2. Does it make sense to feel guilty about our sinful actions? Why or why not?

3. You might believe that God forgives all of our sin through faith in Jesus. But are there any sins that still feel unforgivable to you? Or do you ever feel like you, personally, are unforgivable?

4. What is the difference between being guilty and feeling guilty? Can you feel guilty for something you have not done or that has already been paid for?

5. Do you believe that God is powerful enough — that Jesus' death on the cross for your sin was powerful enough — to take the fact of your guilt for your sin away? Why or why not?

6. If you are a Christian — if you believe God is powerful enough to forgive sin through faith in Jesus' death for sin on the cross — why do you think our feelings of guilt don't always match the fact that we have been made guiltless in God's eyes?

7. What are some Bible verses that can help you remember the fact of God's forgiveness? Use these verses to tell your feelings the truth that you have been forgiven. (Look back through the chapter for many examples. Don't be afraid to underline the best ones.)

8. The Bible tells us that God gives us credit for Jesus' perfect, sinless life when we trust in Christ. Would you rather be judged on Jesus' performance or your own? Why?

9. If someone told you they could never be loved or used by God because of the sinful things they had done, what would you tell them?

10. Do you know anyone who has done some truly terrible things who is now being used by God in new and powerful ways? Why is that possible?

CHAPTER 6

YOUR FINAL CHAPTER
BECOMES A PREFACE

1. What's the scariest thing about dying? Why?

2. How many people have you known personally who have died? Has their experience of death changed how you feel about it?

3. Do you ever think about your own death? Does it frighten you?

4. Can you think of any hero stories in which the hero dies (or appears to die or pretends to die) and then comes back to life? Name one or two of them.

5. Is there any point to Christianity if Jesus did not come back to real, physical life from the dead? (See 1 Corinthians 15:12 – 19 to see how the apostle Paul answered this question.)

6. Why does it matter so much that Jesus was raised from the dead after dying on the cross?

7. Do you ever think about coming back from the dead yourself, about being resurrected? How does that change how you feel about death?

8. Would you rather live forever in the life and body you have now or be raised from the dead to a new life and body in eternity? Why?

9. If we believe that those who are in Christ go on to their best life ever after they die, why are we still so sad? Is it okay for us to feel that way?

10. If you've ever been to an amazing memorial service for someone who was a Christian, talk about what made it so exciting and meaningful.

CHAPTER 7

POWER MOVES IN

1. For God to be God, he has to be powerful. What are some stories from the Bible, history, and your own life in which you see his power?

2. Imagine you are Peter, sitting outside Jesus' trial. How would you have reacted in that moment? (Really think about it.) Now think about what Peter became after Jesus' resurrection — complete confidence. How do you see God doing "Peter-sized changes" in your life?

3. Although Jesus became fully human, he was also fully God. He had supernatural power. Why does it matter that he showed who he was by using that power to do miracles while he was here on earth?

4. How would Jesus' story be different, do you think, if he had never showed that he had the power of God (because he is God)?

5. We read from the Bible in this chapter that when Jesus left earth, he promised to send supernatural power to his followers through the Holy Spirit. What are some of the things Christians can do with that power?

6. In the Bible, God tells us how he wants Christians to live. Do you ever feel like those commands are just too hard?

7. Why do you think we try to live the life God asks us to using only our own power?

8. What are some areas of life in which you've noticed God giving you the power to do what he wants you to do or to feel what he wants you to feel?

9. In what areas of your life do you feel like you could use more of God's power to do what he wants you to do?

10. Can you think of anyone you know whom you have seen change from being weak in some areas to being strong in the way that God wants us to be? If so, talk about what that change looked like.

CHAPTER 8

THE RIGHT DOORS
OPEN

1. Can you think of a time in your life when what you wanted to happen seemed impossible, but then everything lined up just perfectly to make it come together? Tell that story.

2. Think of a time (maybe it's going on right now) when something that seemed like it would be a really good thing just wasn't happening. All of the circumstances of your life seemed to be lining up to keep it from happening. Now tell that story.

3. How much do you think God has to do with our circumstances coming together to open or close the doors to where we want to go? Do you believe he is involved in opening and closing doors?

4. What are some reasons that God may open or close doors to the things we want to do, even things that seem like they would be good? Can we ever really know what those reasons are?

5. Have you ever noticed someone become angry or dis-appointed with God because of a closed door in that person's life? Can you understand why someone would feel that way?

6. Can you think of a time when you were not able to do what you wanted and then later realized that if you *had* done what you wanted, things would have turned out worse for you? Talk about that story.

7. How can God saying no to us through a closed door in our circumstances be a loving thing?

8. Have you ever had to tell someone no for their own good? How did that feel?

9. Does an open door—or the ability to go in a particu-lar direction—automatically mean that's what God wants for you? How can you know the difference?

10. Are there any open doors in your life right now that you feel God is asking you to walk through? What is holding you back?

CHAPTER 9
ALL THINGS WORK
FOR GOOD

1. In the story of your life so far, how big of a role has God played? How involved has he been in the plot, in the major moments, in the darkest days?

2. Do you believe God has been involved in all of your life? Do you believe he has been there every moment, acting out of his love for you? Why or why not?

3. When you believe God is involved in every moment of your life, how does it change the way you think about your story?

4. This chapter talks about one of the famous verses written by the apostle Paul: "And we know that in all things God works for the good of those who love him, who have been called according to his purpose" (Romans 8:28). How do you feel about this verse when you think of some of the hardest parts of your life or the lives of other people who have gone through hard times?

5. Do you remember any of the hard times in Paul's life after he became a Christian and started teaching people about Jesus? How many bad things can you name that happened to him? (Check out 2 Corinthians 11:23–29 if you want an exhaustive list.)

6. If all of those things happened to Paul, how could he write what he did in Romans 8:28?

7. Do you believe God is all three of these things: powerful, good, and loving? Why or why not?

8. Have you noticed God working for your good or someone else's good even in the middle of really hard things? Tell a story about that.

9. What happens to your confidence about the story of your life when you believe that God is at work for good in all the details, even on the hardest days?

10. How will you determine whether your life has been "good" or not?

CHAPTER 10
GOD WILL COME FOR YOU

1. Can a story be good if it doesn't have a good ending?

2. What are some of your favorite endings to stories, books, or movies that you really liked? What made the ending so good?

3. Can you name any movies or books that you were enjoying until they were ruined by the ending?

4. Is the ending to God's story, to your story, really an ending? Why or why not?

5. How is the ending to God's story, to your story, as described in this chapter, also a beginning?

6. What will be the best part of Jesus' return: the ending of this part of the story of all of history?

7. Does the idea of Jesus' return scare you at all? Does it excite you?

8. How does knowing that Jesus is coming back change the way you live from day to day? Should it change how we live?

9. How does it feel to know that one day everyone will understand that Jesus really is the Son of God, that we were right to believe in him? Do you think you will feel vindicated or sad for those who did not believe?

10. Does knowing this day is coming motivate you to tell people about Jesus, about how faith in him has saved you from the consequences that will be faced by those who must pay for their sins on their own?

CONCLUSION
YOU WILL FINALLY GRADUATE

1. Did reading this chapter make you feel emotional at all? Why do you think that is?

2. Do the best stories always have happy endings? Why or why not?

3. Does it scare you a little to be hopeful for the happy ending of heaven and your eternity with God? Why or why not?

4. For you personally, what do you imagine will be the best part of graduating from this life to the eternal one?

5. Do you ever wish the next life would get here more quickly? Do you ever feel lonely for that life, for being with God?

6. What are the best parts of your life right now? Which of those things will continue in eternity and which do you think will be left behind? Why?

7. What are the most difficult parts of your life right now, the ones that will definitely be completely gone when you get to eternity?

8. Have you lost any loved ones who were Christians whom you look forward to being with in eternity with God? What do you imagine it might be like to see them again?

9. If God is involved in all of the details of your story, including your eternity in heaven with him, do you think that eternity will be perfectly satisfying to you?

10. Does knowing that he has prepared a forever home for you make it easier to trust God in the middle of this messy life? Why or why not?

NOTES

1. Ted Gup, "Hard Times, a Helping Hand," *New York Times*, December 22, 2008, www.nytimes.com/2008/12/22/opinion/22gup.html (September 27, 2010).

2. Cited in Richard Mayhue, *Unmasking Satan: Understanding Satan's Battle Plan and Biblical Strategies for Fighting Back* (Grand Rapids: Kregel, 2001), 22.

3. Martin Luther, "A Mighty Fortress Is Our God" (1529), *Lyrics Era*: www.lyricsera.com/433137-lyric-Religious+Music-A+Mighty+Fortress+Is+Our+God.html (October 1, 2010).

4. See A. E. Le Roy, "The Great Barrier Island," in *Journal of the Auckland-Waikato Historical Societies* (April 1978), *Great Barrier Island Tourist Directory*: www.thebarrier.co.nz/History/AELeRoy.htm (October 1, 2010).

5. See Charles Walcott, "Magnetic Orientation in Homing Pigeons," in *IEEE Transactions on Magnetics* 16 (September 1980): 1008–13, *IEEEXplore*: ieeexplore.ieee.org/xpl/freeabs_all.jsp?arnumber=1060868 (October 1, 2010).

6. Cited in John Gilmore, *Probing Heaven* (Grand Rapids: Baker, 1989), 65.

7. Paul Stokes, "Blinded Pilot Guided to Safe Landing by RAF" (© Telegraph Media Group Limited 2008; used by permission), *Telegraph.co.uk* (November 7, 2008), www.telegraph.co.uk/news/newstopics/howaboutthat/3400429/Blinded-pilot-guided-to-safe-landing-by-RAF.html (October 1, 2010).

8. "Sweat Lodge Death Investigation Turns to Self-Help Guru James Arthur Ray" (October 12, 2009), *CBS News*: www.cbsnews.com/8301-504083_162-5378668-504083.html (September 14, 2010); Mike Fleeman, "James Arthur Ray arrested in Sweat Lodge Deaths" (February 3, 2010), *People*: www.people.com/article/0,,20341429,00.html (September 14, 2010).

9. In the NIV, "Son of Man" appears eighty-two times in the Gospels. In Luke 24:7 the angels use the term to refer to Jesus, and in John 12:34 the crowd quotes Jesus describing himself as the Son of Man and asks what the name means. Twice in Mark's narrative (8:31; 9:9), Mark uses the term in paraphrasing Jesus' words.

10. John 8:12; 6:35; 11:25; 14:6 (NKJV); 8:58.

11. James Stalker, *The Life of Christ* (1880; repr., Arlington Heights, Ill.: Christian Liberty, 2002), 82.

12. Quoted in J. John and Chris Walley, *The Life: A Portrait of Jesus* (Milton Keynes, UK: Authentic Media, 2003), 126.

13. "Blind pilot guided to land by RAF" (November 7, 2010), *BBC News*: news.bbc.co.uk/2/hi/uk_news/england /north_yorkshire/7715345.stm; the audio account is embedded in the article (September 14, 2010).

14. "Tennessee Drunk Driving Laws," *Edgar Snyder & Associates*, www.edgarsnyder.com/drunk-driving/statute-limitations/tennessee-drunk-driving-laws.html (September 14, 2010).

15. Cited in Bryan Chapell, *The Promises of Grace: Living in the Grip of God's Love* (1992; repr., Grand Rapids: Baker, 2001), 142. Note: This report was disputed by some authorities.

16. Martin Luther, quoted in Donald G. Bloesch, *Essentials of Evangelical Theology* (San Francisco: HarperSanFrancisco, 1978), 1:148.

17. The story is told in Jon Krakauer, *Into the Wild* (New York: Anchor, 1996), 80–84.

18. Fred Carl Kuehner, "Heaven or Hell," in *Fundamentals of the Faith*, ed. Carl F. H. Henry (Grand Rapids: Zondervan, 1969), 233.

19. Based on mortality rates from "The World Factbook," last updated September 29, 2010, *Central Intelligence Agency*: www.cia.gov/library/publications/the-world-factbook/geos/xx.html (October 1, 2010). The figures are based on estimates of 8.37 deaths per 1,000 population (2009 estimate) and a world population of 6,768,181,146 (July 2010 estimate).

20. Mark 9:31 NKJV; see also 8:31; 10:33–34; 14:28

21. "Theology: The God Is Dead Movement" (October 25, 1965), *Time*: www.time.com/time/magazine/article /0,9171,941410–3,00.html (September 14, 2010).

22. Chaz Corzine, e-mail message to author, August 3, 2010. Used by permission.

23. Billy Graham, "Remarks by Dr. Billy Graham at Richard Nixon's Funeral" (April 27, 1994), *Watergate.info*: www .watergate.info/nixon/94-04-27_funeral-graham.shtml (September 14, 2010).

24. Cited in Jeff Strite, "The Power of Persistent Prayer," *SermonCentral.com*: www.sermoncentral.com/sermons/ the-power-of-persistent-prayer-jeff-strite-sermon-on-prayer-how-to-49222.asp (September 14, 2010).

25. Mark Schlabach, "Injury Swipes McCoy's One Goal" (January 7, 2010), *ESPN*: sports.espn.go.com/ncf/bowls09/ columns/story?columnist=schlabach_mark&id=4807219 (September 15, 2010); "Colt McCoy Postgame Interview

Video: 'I Would Have Given Everything to Be Out There'" (March 18, 2010), *The Huffington Post*: www .huffingtonpost.com/2010/01/08/colt-mccoy-postgame-inter_n_415841.html (October 1, 2010).

26. Edward Mote, "My Hope Is Built on Nothing Less" (1834), *Hymns*: www.hymns.me.uk/my-hope-is-built-on-nothing-less-favorite-hymn.htm (October 28, 2010); put to music in 1863 by composer William Bradbury.

27. David Aikman, *Great Souls: Six Who Changed the Century* (Nashville: Word, 1998), 78. Many of the details of Mandela's life described in this chapter are taken from pages 61 – 123 of *Great Souls*.

28. Aikman, *Great Souls*, 108.

29. Aikman, *Great Souls*, 116, 64.

30. Figures vary widely. The figure 106 billion is cited by Carl Haub, "How Many People Have Ever Lived on Earth" (November/December 2002), *Population Reference Bureau*: www.prb.org/Articles/2002/HowMany PeopleHaveEverLivedonEarth.aspx (October 1, 2010).

31. Cited in Paul Lee Tan, *Encyclopedia of 7700 Illustrations: Signs of the Times* (Rockville, Md.: Assurance, 1988), #5470.

32. Joni Eareckson Tada, *Heaven: Your Real Home* (Grand Rapids: Zondervan, 1995), 41.

GOD'S STORY
your story

The Story: Teen Edition

The Bible as One Continuing Story of God and His People

"The Greatest Story Ever Told" is more than just a cliché. God has gone to great lengths to rescue lost and hurting people. That is what *The Story: Teen Edition* is all about—the story of the Bible, God's great love affair with humanity. Condensed into 31 accessible chapters, *The Story: Teen Edition* sweeps you into the unfolding progression of Bible characters and events from Genesis to Revelation. Using the clear, accurate, and easy-to-understand text of the New International Version, it allows the stories, poems, and teachings of the Bible to read like a novel. And like any good story, it is filled with intrigue, drama, conflict, romance, and redemption.

Available in stores and online!

The Story, Teen Curriculum

Finding Your Place in the Story of God

Lessons Written by Michael Novelli

Using the clear text of the New International Version, this rendering of the Bible allows its stories, poems, and teachings to come together in a single, compelling experience. *The Story, Teen Edition* sweeps you into the unfolding progression of Bible characters and events from Genesis to Revelation. And, like any good story, it is filled with intrigue, drama, conflict, romance, and redemption.

This DVD, a companion to *The Story, Teen Edition* print book, helps teens understand *The Story* more clearly through experiential learning. Michael Novelli has seen that when teens experience a story, as opposed to it being told or shown to them, they absorb and remember it more thoroughly. This DVD offers youth workers a new way to engage teens in the grand narrative of the Bible.

Available in stores and online!

ZONDERVAN®
.com

Every christian has a story to tell.
His Is Mine.com makes it possible

HIS IS MINE

Whether new or lifelong, bold or quiet, obvious or subtle, each person's story of Christian belief is unique, moving, inspiring, and passionate, and carries a desire for that same God-connection in the hearts of others.

The "His Is Mine" (H.I.M.) campaign, inspired by Max Lucado's book, *God's Story, Your Story*, enables the body of Christ to unite, be heard, and reflect the power of God's story in millions of individuals' lives. It's a powerful initiative intended to create a movement with significant and eternal outcomes.

To get started, visit **HisIsMine.com** and tell your salvation story using the format you are most comfortable with: video, audio, or text. Once uploaded, you can share your story or any other on the site to saturate the online world with the transforming power of Jesus Christ.

Join us! Share your "His Is Mine" story. It may be yours that inspires others to find theirs—to make God's story their own.

▶HisIsMine.com

Talk It Up!

Want free books?
First looks at the best new fiction?
Awesome exclusive merchandise?

We want to hear from you!

Give us your opinions on titles, covers, and stories.
Join the Z Street Team.

Email us at zstreetteam@zondervan.com
to sign up today!

Also—Friend us on Facebook!

www.facebook.com/goodteenreads

- Video Trailers
- Connect with your favorite authors
- Sneak peeks at new releases
- Giveaways
- Fun discussions
- And much more!